How to
Repair Food

How to Repair Food

Marina and John Bear

with Tanya Zeryck

TEN SPEED PRESS
Berkeley, California

Ten Speed Press
P.O. Box 7123
Berkeley, California 94707

Distributed in Australia by Simon and Schuster Australia, in Canada
by Publishers Group West, in New Zealand by Tandem Press, in
South Africa by Real Books, in Southeast Asia by Berkeley Books,
and in the United Kingdom and Europe by Airlift Books.

Cover design by Fifth Street Design
Interior design by Jeff Brandenburg, ImageComp

Library of Congress Cataloging-in-Publication Data

Bear, Marina, 1941–
    How to repair food / by Marina & John Bear with Tanya Zeryck.
        p.   cm.
    ISBN 0–89815–555–X
    1. Cookery.   I. Bear, John, 1938–   . II. Zeryck, Tanya.
    III. Title.
    TX652.B34   1998
    641.5—dc21   98–6444
                                                            CIP

First printing this edition, 1998
Printed in Canada

1 2 3 4 5 6 7 8 9 10 — 02 01 00 99 98

"If this is coffee, please bring me some tea.
But if this is tea, please bring me some coffee."

—*Abraham Lincoln*

Contents

Introduction

There are thousands of cookbooks in the world, and they are all, at heart, the same.

They tell you how to cook.

This book is different.

It tells you how to correct mistakes. It tells you how to undo whatever it is you have done that you wish you hadn't done. It tells you what to do about fallen cakes, salty soups, burned stews, overcooked cauliflower, and hundreds of other things that can happen even to the best of cooks. It tells you, in other words, how to repair food. (Say, that would make a good title!)

When your car breaks down, you don't throw it away. You find an expert in car repair.

When your washing machine fails, you don't throw it away. You find an expert in appliance repair.

And yet most people who have kitchen failures throw the food away. There is no need. This book is devoted to the art and practice of food repair.

Read the preface or introduction to your favorite cookbook. The chances are you'll find a paragraph something like this:

Importance of Following Instructions

Each recipe in this book has been carefully tested and checked for accuracy. It is important that you follow instructions *exactly*. Be sure you measure ingredients *carefully*, and time your cooking *precisely*. This is the only way you can guarantee perfect results every time.

Fine. We agree. Makes lots of sense.

But among all those thousands of cookbooks, have you ever seen a single one that tells you what to do when:

1. The doorbell rings and, while you're paying postage due to the letter carrier, the cauliflower overcooks and turns mushy.

2. You're not wearing your glasses, and you set the burner too high, and the baked beans have stuck to the pot and burned.

3. The cheese you were going to put in the casserole has gone moldy.

4. The telephone rings while you're making the gravy and, by the time you get back, it's gone all lumpy (the gravy, not the telephone).

5. The only loaf of bread in the house is stale, and the school bus is due soon, and you have to make those sandwiches for the kids.

6. The stew is simmering away, and you sample it, and it tastes more like junior-high lunch special than beef bourguignon.

7. You put salt in the vegetable soup and forgot you did, and then you put it in again, and now it's much too salty.

8. Your invitation said dinner would be served promptly at seven and it's half past six, and you find you didn't put the potatoes in with the roast.

9. They had this fantastic special at the store, and you went mad, and now you have five heads of lettuce sitting there, wilting.

10. Your spouse unexpectedly brings his or her boss home for dinner, and there just won't be enough chicken to go around.

And so on. And so on. And so on.

In other words, those other cookbooks simply do not tell you how to correct mistakes. None of them tells you how to undo the damage that you, or the supermarket, or Mother Nature, or the cow have already done.

This book does.

This book tells you what to do when you discover that just about any kind of food, drink, or utensil is overcooked, undercooked, stale, spoiled, burned, lumpy, salty, peppery, bland, too spicy, too hot, too cold, moldy, frozen, gamey, fuzzy, mushy, too dry, too wet, flat, tough, too thick, too thin, wilted, fatty, collapsed, exploded, shriveled, curdled, cracked, scaly, smelly, greasy, dirty, stringy, twiggy, mealy, clogged, or stuck together.

This book is *How to Repair Food*.

It first appeared thirty years ago, and it's still unique. This edition has been thoroughly updated. It's amazing how much our eating patterns have changed in the last thirty years. Remember when a Diet Plate was a scoop of (full fat) cottage cheese, a hamburger patty (lots of protein for you dieters!), a slice of tomato, and a canned peach half? But the basics of kitchen catastrophes haven't changed all that much. Things still get overcooked, lumpy, dry, and stuck. What's changed in this edition reflects how we expect food to look these days. Thirty years ago, you could pour hollandaise sauce on a skimpy pile of asparagus and your guests would think "cuisine." Nowadays, they think "heart attack."

The intervening years have given us one more great option for food repair, however. Presentation has become much more important than quantity. Those four spears of asparagus can be tied together with a strip of red cabbage, red bell pepper, a thin twist of lemon peel or, what the heck, all three, and yet again your guests will think "cuisine."

Note in Passing

In the preparation of this book, we looked at more than 2,000 different cookbooks to see what, if anything, they had to say about repairing food. Not one acknowledged the need to do so. They all just assume that everything will always be perfect. These books, incidentally, fall into one of five basic categories:

First, there are the Businesslike Cookbooks. They have businesslike titles, such as *Basic Culinary Techniques*, or *Mrs. Rutherford's Cooking Academy Cookbook*. They simply tell you how to cook. And of course if you follow their directions, nothing will ever go wrong.

Second, there are the Specialized Cookbooks: *The Cranberry Cookbook, The Romance of Arugula, Cooking from the Highlands of Tibet, 1,001 Tempting Recipes for Leftover Okra*. But all they do is tell you how to cook cranberries, or yaks, or whatever. Never how to repair things.

Third, there are the Expensive Gimmicky Cookbooks, made either to be given as gifts or to be left on your coffee table. No one has ever been known to buy one for personal use—books like *Favorite Recipes of the Postmasters General* or *Armand's Cafe Boeuf Cuisine* (where all the pictures are full-page artsy shots of Armand's hands knitting a crown roast together or arranging the garnish on his Shanks à la Shanghai). These books don't help you when something goes wrong— unless you can be consoled by looking at full-color glossy photos of magnificent food.

Fourth, there are the Anecdotal Cookbooks, which tend to be travel books, joke books, and/or autobiographies, with some recipes thrown in: *Through Darkest Venezuela with Sterno and Toothpick, Take It Off, Take It Off (It's Boiling Over)*, the warm, witty story of Zizi LaFleur, Queen of Burlesque and Queen of the Kitchen. Anecdotes aside, these books tell you how to cook, but never what to do when what you cooked needs to be repaired.

And finally there is the unending flow of Folksy Cookbooks, in which someone has finally persuaded Aunt Bessie, or Mrs. Mugglesby of Daisy Hill Farm, to record for posterity all their famous receipts (which is the folksy word for recipe). So we have *Aunt Bessie's Own Cookbook* and *The Eatin's Good on Daisy Hill.* Presumably Aunt Bessie never made mistakes. If she did, she ain't talkin'.

How This Book Is Organized

The major part of the text consists of an alphabetical listing of all foods and then, under each specific food, another alphabetical listing of the things that might go wrong, and how to repair them.

For example, we have:

ASPARAGUS

Bland

Frozen to box

Not enough

Old

Overcooked

Thawed

Too much

Of course the subcategories will differ for each food; no two foods have an identical array of potential problems. Some problems you run into may simply not be listed. There are two good reasons for this:

1. Not every problem has a solution—or has, in fact, been identified. Who knows, you may be the first person in the history of the world to be suffering from stringy yogurt.

2. Not every solution is known to us. We did a lot of research, both in libraries and in our own kitchen, but there must be some things we have overlooked.

This edition reflects some of the problems people have thrown at us (figuratively) over the years and the answers we've been able to come up with to solve them. But the quest for alternatives to dumping your food disasters continues. Please send us your problems, questions, suggestions, and solutions, and we'll do our best to treat them kindly. Write to Marina and John Bear, Ten Speed Press, P.O. Box 7123, Berkeley, CA 94707, and realize that publishers are well-intentioned, but often take an amazingly long time to forward mail to authors. Thank you.

When you *don't* find the answer to your problem in this book, you may well wish to improvise, bluff, or otherwise muddle through. To assist you in this process, when the need arises (and it will, it will), we have included a brief section entitled "How to Improvise, Bluff, or Otherwise Muddle Through." Here you will find some general philosophy, along with a list of basic ingredients for a kitchen "first aid kit"—foods that can be used in different ways to help solve a variety of problems.

Also, there are some corrective techniques that apply not to a single specific food or problem, but to a wide range of foods. For instance, there are things you can do about burned foods that work equally well with burned green beans, burned stew, or burned pudding. The same is true for frozen foods that have thawed out before you wanted them to. So, for advice relevant to these situations—burning and thawing—see Appendices A and B at the back of the book.

There are other appendices back there, too, dealing with measuring, pouring, seasonability of foods, stain removal, and so forth.

Appendix H deserves special mention. It is called "Problems with Utensils and Appliances" and deals with situations ranging from burned pots to clogged grinders. It even covers those handy utensils you carry around on the ends of your arms: what to do about burned, greasy, smelly, and stained hands.

This edition of *How to Repair Food* was revised as a joint effort by one of its original authors (Marina Bear) and the daughter of the original authors (Tatiana Bear Zeryck), who lives across the country from her parents (thus bringing a wider perspective to a whole range of cooking topics from availability of food products to current dietary and health concerns). Tanya was the younger co-author who pointed out, in addressing the problem of bland foods that advice on improving bland vegetables often involves adding something to the cooking water "from the beginning." But how do you know foods are bland until the end? (This tends to be the sort of thing that is annoyingly common in cookbooks. How many times does one read a recipe for, say, a frittata that says to add salt "to taste" to the egg mixture. Do people really scoop up spoonfuls of raw egg to taste?) Let's deal with that one right here. Sometimes you don't know until the end of the cooking period that your corned beef, for example, is bland. We're not going to tell you to serve it with mustard or Cajun hot sauce. We're sure you could figure that possibility out. But next time you make that brand of corned beef, you'll know how to make the experience more satisfying for all concerned.

One more thing.

Into every cook's life there comes Total Failure.

Sometimes twice a week.

Total Failure is a different kind of situation from any of the others we discuss, so we have given it a special section, just before the start of the alphabetical listings.

We hope you'll never need to use this book—in much the same way we hope you'll never need to see a doctor or a car mechanic. But we also hope you will agree, in all three cases, that you're kind of glad they're there.

How to Improvise, Bluff, or Otherwise Muddle Through

This is the Great Encouragement section. This is the place you go when the main course has turned gray, when the dessert hasn't jelled yet, when there's a funny smell in the house and you discover it is coming from the kitchen.

Or, more specifically, come back to this section when you have a specific problem that isn't covered in the main part of the text.

Our message is Take heart! When everything seems to be going wrong—or has, in fact, gone wrong—it is still possible to snatch victory (and your dinner) from the very jaws of defeat and the garbage can. You need only courage, a bit of creativity (yours or ours), and a good set of "first aid" ingredients for repairing damaged food.

Here, then, is a list of emergency supplies that should equip you to weather a wide variety of kitchen catastrophes. And in case everything goes wrong, it is even possible to create an entirely satisfactory dinner for four out of emergency supplies you squirrel away just in case. See Appendix F for details.

First Aid Supplies

Dried onions. No one ever expects to run out of fresh onions. Everyone does at least 4.7 times a year. Dried onions are a natural for helping to fill out anemic soups and stews (add 2 tablespoons of sautéed dried onions for each cup of liquid). They will add flavor to almost any bland vegetable, make an interesting topping for a casserole when combined with crushed potato chips or cornflakes, or even make blah sandwiches unexpectedly good (how about dried onions, browned or not, with cheese, or peanut butter, or tuna fish?).

Grated Parmesan cheese. The ideal hurry-up topping. Parmesan hides a multitude of sins when used as a casserole topping and tastes good on most cooked vegetables, fish, and poultry. Don't forget a good sprinkling on a salad that needs something.

Instant vanilla pudding. A dessert's salvation. You can pad out skimpy pie fillings by using the pudding as a base layer, with the fruit on top. You can use it as a sauce over insufficient quantities of fruit or cake. You can even use it, we are told, to make vanilla pudding.

Hollandaise sauce (cans or packages). These days, you don't need much. Everybody knows it's sinfully rich and difficult to make, so a graceful dollop over insufficient vegetables can make a big difference. Same goes for fish and eggs. Use it straight, or add a pinch of tarragon and you have béarnaise sauce for meat, fish, or vegetables. Add some tomato sauce (2 teaspoons per can of hollandaise) and you have choron sauce for eggs or meat. Adding ½ tablespoon of grated orange zest and 2 tablespoons of orange juice and you have maltaise sauce, which will make the most tasteless fish or vegetable into something exotic.

Cheese sauce or cheese soup. One can is instant help for some dry casseroles. Pour it on vegetables. Heat it up and pour it on toast for instant Welsh rarebit.

Clam chowder. Find a good brand that's short on potatoes and long on clams. It makes a good first course (when you're faced with less main course than you think you need). Not bad for snacks or lunch, and it's a key ingredient in the emergency meal in Appendix F.

Baking soda. Never let your kitchen be without it. Besides its cooking, medicinal, stain removing, and deodorizing uses (you probably already have an open box of it in the fridge), it is the ideal kitchen fire extinguisher—especially for grease fires. Simply pour lots on a fire. Note: Trying to douse a grease fire with water will normally only make things worse.

Lemon juice. Keep a bottle of the reconstituted stuff in your fridge. Lemon juice livens up older vegetables and doubtful fishes. Use it whenever something is darkening that shouldn't: fruit slices, avocados, parsnips, etc. If you don't want the end product to have a lemony taste, rinse whatever-it-is under gently running cold water before going on. You can even make lemonade for unexpected company.

Prepared baking mix. There is old reliable Bisquick. There is a lighter (less fat) version. There are even convenience baking mixes in your natural food store. For fast-baked foods, from cookies and coffeecake to quick breads and biscuits, it is often very comforting to know that you are not more than 13 minutes away from something homemade.

Mashed potato flakes. Mashed potato flakes are not just for mashed potatoes. They are a fast and nutritious thickener for soups and stews. Just add them by the handful until you've got the consistency you want. Also, they are a great extender for most vegetables. Chop up the vegetable (for instance, carrots, beans, broccoli) after it is cooked and well drained. Combine it with an equal amount of reconstituted mashed potatoes. Top this with Parmesan cheese and run it under the broiler for 2 or 3 minutes, until the top is browned.

Couscous (or rice). Look in the rice section of your store for couscous. Chances are overwhelming you will find a box of instant couscous. Buy it and save it, unless you're not familiar with couscous. In that case, buy two and try one. It's a great "underneath" for meat, fish, or vegetable stews. It's exotic enough that it looks special, but tastes simple and supportive. If you can't find it (or you or the two-year-old you live with won't try new stuff), then substitute quick-cooking rice, which even comes in brown nowadays.

Artichoke hearts (quartered). If you have room in your freezer, keep a couple of boxes of frozen artichoke hearts in the back corner. They are unusual enough that they look special, and they're one of the few vegetables that stand up well to preserving. You can stack a couple of cans of them in the back of the cupboard, if the freezer is full (be sure they're not the marinated kind that usually come in jars). They make a great addition to an insufficient salad and are part of the emergency meal in Appendix F.

Garbanzo beans. Also known as chickpeas. Beans are the other kind of vegetable matter that isn't diminished by canning processes. These are great salad and main-course enhancers, because they're filling and nutritious and interesting looking, while being fairly bland and adaptable, tastewise.

Sun-dried tomatoes. If you can find the kind packed in olive oil, get those. The oil goes well in a salad or a pasta topping. Otherwise, get the kind in a plastic pouch and leave it unopened until you really need them. Long-term vegetables are hard to find, and these are good to get to know. They taste good, and they're sort of the pimiento of the nineties—the cheery red bits in casseroles, the spot of color in the garnish, the interesting flavor in the emergency meal salad.

Canned shrimp. This is the basis for any number of emergency responses. It can be added to soup, to a salad, or to a casserole. It can inspire quick appetizers or make a good sandwich filling. It's part of the emergency meal, though, so remember to replace your supply when you grab it for a late-night snack.

Unflavored gelatin. For thickening cool things unflavored gelatin works wonders. Soften a package in ¼ cup of cold water and add it to 1 cup of warm liquid to dissolve it. Then add to aspic, pudding, pie filling (cooked), or whatever. It will even rescue a soggy croquette, if that's your problem (see **croquettes**). It is also a pretty good start for a lot of fancy desserts. Check any good cookbook, or improvise.

Good sherry. Like hollandaise, sherry is a gourmet touch that can turn a disaster into a triumph. It makes any stew, soup, or casserole taste richer. Start with 2 tablespoons in a four- to six-person potful, let it simmer (or bake) for a few minutes, and taste. You can sprinkle it on a variety of desserts, from pudding to cake. And you can always serve it straight (or over ice) to your starving guests while you're busy patching things up in the kitchen.

Evaporated milk. Next shopping list, add a 12-ounce can. How many times have you run out of milk in the last two years? See? Use evaporated milk anywhere you'd use whole milk by adding an equal amount of water (so a 12-ounce can makes 3 cups of milk): desserts, sauces, baths, etc. You can use it to make a whipped topping. And there are low-fat and fat-free versions, too. Choose your favorite.

Basic spices and spice mixes. A basic spice is one you can add to almost anything with some likelihood of improving and/or making more interesting the anything. Everybody has his or her own basics. Ours are the following:

chile powder and Italian herbs (depending on whether we feel Mexican or Italian)

cinnamon (try it in entrées as well as in desserts and drinks)

curry powder

fines herbes

garlic salt or powder (powder is stronger; salt is saltier)

fresh pepper

We've recently found a Thai spice mix that does nice and unexpected things to savory dishes and a Cajun spice powder in a round canister that is so good that it might be addictive.

The basic rule of thumb on herbs and spices is to add ¼ teaspoon for each pound of ingredients, and then start tasting. Use this amount throughout the suggestions in this book, unless we advise otherwise or your own preferences say something else. Some foods will require much more spice than this; others (especially if you use cloves and saffron, for instance) will need less. Improvise and experiment with whatever you have on hand. And write down what you do, in case you come up with something great.

Food colorings. Big secret. A few drops of yellow in the curried rice or the biscuit dough makes it look richer. A pallid soup can be reddened a little and made much more appetizing. (Sure, you could grate a little fresh beet into the soup, but do you have a fresh beet on hand? Good. Then do that instead.) And then there's the blue mashed potatoes and the green scrambled eggs the kids are still telling their friends about.

You may ordinarily keep some of these things on hand. Buy the others and tuck them away in an emergency corner of the cupboard. They all have a very long shelf life. Sometimes true happiness is remembering you have a can of chickpeas stashed away.

Let us repeat, because we cannot say it often enough: Improvise! That is the key to success when something goes wrong. Think of it this way: What have you got to lose? As far as is known, there are no two foods that, when mixed together, will explode. The worst that can happen is that a partial disaster may be converted into a total disaster—perhaps even a glorious disaster, one your grandchildren will remember and discuss with awe.

And you may have surprising success. Look, if the Mexicans can serve poultry with chocolate sauce and the Uruguayans can improve a steak by spreading peanut butter on it, surely there is something you can do with that quivering mass in your kitchen that looks like the poster from Invasion of the Killer Casseroles.

Total Failure

When you have a total, absolute, cannot-be-corrected, you've-tried-to-improvise-and-only-made-it-worse failure, there are three, and only three, paths open to you.

The first is run yourself through with your sword. This may seem a bit extreme for a culinary bungle, but there is good historical precedent: the case of François Vâtel, steward to the French minister of finance under Louis XIV, whom many still regard as one of the Top Ten Chefs of all time.

One day King Louis XIV came calling. Vâtel prepared a great meal, but the king's party was larger than expected and there wasn't enough food to go around. Some had to make do with boiled eggs, or the like.

Vâtel was disconsolate, but he vowed to redeem himself the following day, which happened to be a Friday. Fresh fish was a rarity in those days, and Vâtel had placed orders with fishermen throughout the region. Late that night he was called to the kitchen to accept delivery from one of the fishermen. He did not realize that this was only a small part of his order. "Is that all there is?" he asked in disbelief. "Yes," he was mistakenly told.

One failure was enough. Two in a row were literally unbearable. Vâtel went up to his room and ran himself through with his sword. He was found dead a short time later, when someone came to tell him that the rest of the fish had arrived.

Now, whatever you've done, it can't be that bad, can it? So please, do not run yourself through with your sword. For that matter, don't even jab yourself with your shrimp deveiner. Try alternatives two or three.

The second alternative is to whip up a gourmet meal in twenty minutes, start to finish, from a simple set of ingredients you already have on hand. This is entirely possible, but only if you have the emergency ingredients described a few pages back. If you believed us when we suggested you keep a kitchen "first aid kit" on hand, turn now to Appendix F (page 123), and you will find a pretty good dinner for four that can be made from scratch in a mere 1200 seconds.

Don't forget to replace any emergency ingredients you may use. We don't want to sound too pessimistic, but, as Mrs. Vâtel may well have said to her husband on Thursday night, "Sleep well, François; who knows what may happen tomorrow?"

The final alternative is to give up entirely and let someone else do the cooking. In other words, go out to dinner. You can deal with the kitchen disaster tomorrow, which is, as Scarlett O'Hara said, another day.

Alphabetical Listings

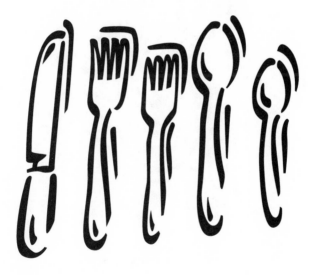

ABALONE: *See also* **FISH AND SEAFOOD**

Tough: After it has been cooked and you find yourself faced with several rejected portions of (terribly expensive) abalone chewing gum, you can still produce abalone chowder. Very elegant.

ABALONE CHOWDER

Tough abalone
4 slices bacon (uncooked), diced
1 medium onion, minced
1 medium potato, diced
1 bottle clam juice
3 cups milk, or 2 of milk and 1 of light cream
2 tablespoons of sherry (optional)
Salt and pepper to taste

Was this your usual breaded slice of abalone? If so, scrape off as much of the breading as you can (but no need to get it all; it will help thicken the soup). Mince the abalone (a food processor will help). Cook the bacon, stirring, in a saucepan until crisp. Remove and reserve the bacon. Put the onions and potatoes into the bacon fat in the saucepan and cook until the onions are golden. Add abalone, clam juice, milk, bacon, and sherry. Heat to simmer and allow to cook 5 minutes. Season with salt and pepper. Serve in warmed bowls.

Next time, you've got to tenderize it more thoroughly. There are two schools of tenderizing. The first says, slice it as thin as you can into big oval slices and pound it with a meat-tenderizing hammer until you can read a newspaper through it and then proceed. The gentle persuasion school says, after trimming off the inedible bits, slice off the "handle" (where it was attached to the shell). You now have two pieces of abalone. Wrap one in a clean kitchen towel and pound it, firmly but not violently, with a rolling pin, working from one end to the other until it "relaxes." This can take a while. Check to be sure you're not whomping it to bits in there. Then do the other piece. Then slice it on the bias into ⅛-inch strips. Good luck.

ALCOHOL: *see also* WINE

For major problems with things alcoholic, please consult the telephone directory for your nearest AA office. Here are a few lesser problems:

Brandy or liqueur won't ignite: It's probably not hot enough. Drain it off if feasible (don't worry if it isn't) and start with new alcohol. Most of the remaining liquor will burn off anyway, so your guests shouldn't get too sozzled—at least not from this dish. Heat alcohol for flaming slowly, over a low flame. (If it gets too hot, it may ignite in the pan. If this happens, pour it on the food right away.) When it's hot, pour it on gently and ignite the *fumes*, not the *liquid.* Say, maybe that was your problem in the first place.

Drink tastes too alcoholy (too strong, etc.): We don't know precisely what this means, but some people, not all of whom come from Iowa, think they do. They tell us that floating a thin slice of cucumber in the drink (or long thin slices of cucumber in the punch bowl) makes it less alcoholy tasting.

Not enough: If you're stuck with a depleted liquor cabinet before dinner, try making quick punch out of fruit juice, whatever you have that's carbonated, and whiskey, rum, brandy, and/or vodka. Doctor it to taste with sugar, lemon, butters, rosemary, nutmeg, and/or whole cardamom.

If it is *between* or *after* meals, things are simpler. Instead of punch, you can make Irish coffee, hot toddies, or brandied grog. Be sure you don't ask people what they want. Come in with the stuff all ready, and those who imbibe are less likely to refuse.

Punch too bland, missing something: Assuming that what is missing is something other than alcohol, here are three seasonings that tend to give punch punch: cardamom, nutmeg, and rosemary. For a punch bowl, stir about 1 teaspoon of rosemary, nutmeg, or powdered cardamom into ½ cup of hot fruit juice. Let it cool to room temperature (or if you're in a hurry, let it sit for 5 minutes and cool it by adding cold juice). Taste test it by adding a bit to a sample of the punch before you dump the whole thing in.

ALMONDS: *see* NUTS

ANCHOVIES

Not enough: In salads, add the oil from the anchovy can to the salad dressing. It will make the salad taste considerably more anchovyful (and also more salty, so be sure to taste before adding any salt.)

In hors d'oeuvres, mash the anchovies up with cream cheese.

In sauces (like spaghetti or pizza sauce), add the oil from the can to the sauce (remember about the salt).

Salty: Soak the anchovies in clear tap water for about 10 minutes. Pat them dry with paper towels. If you don't intend to use them right away, store them in a container with enough olive oil to cover them. (No olive oil? All right, some other kind of cooking oil.)

APPLES, COOKED: *see also* APPLES, RAW

Bland: Sprinkle on some powdered ginger, mace, coriander, cinnamon, and/or add a clove bag (a few whole cloves tied in cheesecloth) to an apple dish and cook it a little longer. Or dump some caraway seeds (mixed with sugar), some fennel, or some grated lemon or orange peel down the hole of a blah baked apple and cook it ten minutes more.

Burned: *See* **Appendix A: BURNED FOODS**

Not enough: If the apples are going to be served with meat, augment them with quartered onions sautéed in a covered saucepan until soft (about 10 minutes) in a tablespoon of butter per medium-sized onion. Add a handful of raisins (optional) that you have plumped in a cup of boiling water and then drained.

If the apples are for dessert, combine them with cranberries or any other kind of berries or pitted cherries or canned pineapple, or add fresh sliced pears when the apples are about half cooked, plus 1 tablespoon of vanilla extract and an extra ⅛ teaspoon of cinnamon. (If you use winter pears, you may have to add more sugar.) You can add canned apricots if you're desperate, but be sure to drain them well, pit them, and then rename your dessert, for the apricots will now be the dominant taste.

APPLES, RAW: *see also* APPLES, COOKED

Bland: Dip sliced or quartered apples, peeled or unpeeled, in powdered anise. Or sprinkle on some powdered cinnamon, nutmeg, and/or poppy seed. In fruit salad, try mashed-up rosemary or powdered cardamom. (Stir ¼ teaspoon of either into ½ cup of honey and spoon it over the apples. Honey too sweet? Use fruit juice instead.) Improvise!

Discoloring: Apples do this when their flesh is exposed to the air. Rub a little lemon juice on the exposed flesh. If it is already unpleasantly dark, cut off the dark layer. No lemon juice? Dunk the apple pieces in slightly salted water until you're ready to use them. Or, if the taste is compatible, submerge them in pineapple juice instead.

Mealy: There is no known way to unmeal an apple. No matter what you were planning to do, make applesauce.

Too Many: If you've overdone it at the roadside stand, you can always make applesauce (it's easy) just to your taste—smooth, chunky, cinnamon, maple syrup–spiked. Consult a basic cookbook.

ARTICHOKE: *see also* ARTICHOKE HEARTS

Bland: The best thing is a tiny, tiny, wee bit of dried fennel (about ⅛ teaspoon) in the cooking water. Once they are fully cooked, you'll have to add flavoring to the butter you dip the leaves in; for instance, a shake of Tabasco sauce in the butter, or use hollandaise sauce or aioli (very garlicky mayonnaise) instead of butter for dipping. Or make instant béarnaise sauce by adding a good pinch of tarragon to the hollandaise. Or use vinaigrette (3 parts oil to 1 part vinegar) on either hot or cold artichokes.

Burned: The only way to burn an artichoke is to boil away all the water. This time, cut away the burned parts, see Appendix H for dealing with burned utensils, and resume cooking.

Next time, use more water. A big potful can't possibly boil away—at least not before the artichoke is hopelessly overcooked. With steamed artichoke: Be careful!

Difficult to drain: Put something absorbent, like a washcloth or lots of paper towels, in the bottom of a bowl. Turn the artichoke upside down in the bowl. (Please clean the washcloth before using it on yourself. If artichoke balm were any good for us, you can be sure the cosmetic people would be selling it.)

Old: If your artichokes have been around a while, add a teaspoon of salt and a half teaspoon of sugar to each quart of water you use to cook them. The sugar sweetens them just a tiny bit (what a surprise!), and the salt helps retain color and flavor.

If your old artichokes look funny, try removing some of the outer leaves. They may still be just fine inside.

Separating, falling apart: Once it has started, there isn't much you can do beyond handling them very carefully. A good way to keep it from happening next time is to wrap the artichokes in cheesecloth before cooking. We suggest you remove the cheesecloth before serving—definitely before eating!

ARTICHOKE HEARTS: *see also* **ARTICHOKE**

Frozen to the box: Run cold water into the box, and after a few seconds the artichokes should dislodge themselves.

Pickledy: Sometimes the marinade favor is so strong it pickles your taste buds and gets in the way of tasting artichoke. Soak the hearts in clear water for 10 minutes, and then, if you aren't going to use them at once, store them covered with olive oil (or, if you have none, some other kind of oil). Guaranteed to be less pickledy.

Thawed: If frozen artichoke hearts have thawed out and you didn't want them to, see Appendix B.

ASPARAGUS

Bland: Add bouillon to the cooking water next time. For now, sprinkle the asparagus with ground mustard seed or sesame seeds—or use seasoned salt, or flavored butter, or tamari soy sauce.

Frozen to the box: Run a bit of cold tap water into the spaces in the carton; the asparagus should loosen up at once.

Not enough: Not a problem. Asparagus displays beautifully in small quantities. If you're serving a special dinner, arrange the spears in a bunch or hold them in the middle and fan out the tips and bottoms. "Tie" the middle with a vegetable ribbon, arranged gracefully: use a thin ribbon of cabbage, lettuce, red bell pepper, chives or scallion—even a shaving of carrot will do. If you're feeding family, make this:

ASPARAGUS RISOTTO

1 small onion, chopped
2 tablespoons olive oil
1 clove garlic, minced
2 cups rice (no short-grain Italian arborio rice? use whatever kind you have)
3½ cups stock or bouillon (any kind)
½ cup cream (or evaporated milk, or half-and-half)
¼ cup Parmesan cheese

1 lonely bunch of asparagus, cut into 2-inch lengths (set the tip pieces aside)
Salt to taste

Cook the onion in the oil in a saucepan, until the onion's soft. Add the garlic and stir in. Add the rice and stir it, over medium heat, for about 5 minutes. Meanwhile, heat up the stock. Pour the heated stock into the rice (it'll sizzle a lot at first). Add the cut-up asparagus stalks (not the tips), stir it all together, lower the heat, and cook ⅔ of the time you need to do the rice (white rice=15 minutes; brown rice=30 minutes). Then add the asparagus tips, the Parmesan, and the cream, and continue to cook until rice is tender. Check for seasoning and salt as needed.

Old: Add a pinch of sugar (for sweetness) and ¼ teaspoon of salt (to help retain color and flavor) to each cup of cooking water.

Overcooked: Easy answer—make soup. If you have a can of cream-of-anything on hand, make it up, chop the overcooked asparagus up, and combine it with the soup. If not, make a cream sauce. Chop the tips of the asparagus up and put them aside. Purée the rest of the asparagus stems in your food processor or blender. Add the white sauce. Put this lovely glop into a saucepan over low heat. Thin to desired consistency with stock or bouillon. Add the reserved chopped tips.

If you have time (and you could by substituting another vegetable for tonight, no?), this recipe is not only great for overcooked asparagus, it's a main course.

TIMBALE D'ASPERGES

½ cup minced onions
¼ teaspoon salt
Pinch of nutmeg
Big pinch of white pepper
½ cup grated cheese (preferably Swiss; any kind will do)
⅔ cup bread crumbs
2 eggs
1 cup milk
1 to 2 cups overcooked asparagus

Sauté onions for 5 minutes. Put them in a large bowl. Add the salt, nutmeg, pepper, cheese, ⅓ cup bread crumbs. Beat in the eggs. Bring the milk to a boil and beat into the mix. Mash the asparagus into the mix. Grease a 2-quart mold or baking pan. Coat it with ⅓ cup bread crumbs. Turn the asparagus mix into the pan. Put that pan into a larger pan on the bottom of your oven. Fill the outer pan with boiling water. Set the oven to about 275° to 300°, to keep the water in the outer pan at a simmer. Bake 30 to 40 minutes, until a knife inserted into the center comes out clean.

Thawed: See Appendix B regarding frozen food that has thawed before you are ready for it.

Too much: Cook it all, refrigerate it, and next day make something else, such as the following:

ORIENTAL SALAD

Chilled asparagus
Lettuce
Roasted red peppers or sweet red peppers
  (or tomatoes, if you must)
Lemon juice
Salad oil
Soy sauce
Sesame seeds

Cut up the chilled asparagus and combine it with the lettuce and red vegetable. Dress with a mixture of 1 part lemon juice to 2 parts salad oil. Add a dash of soy sauce. Cover with about ¼ cup of sesame seeds that have been toasted in a 350° oven on a cookie sheet for 5 minutes.

ASPIC: *see* GELATIN

AVOCADOS

Darkening: The simplest method to inhibit darkening is to restore the avocado meat to the immediate vicinity of the pit. The pit somehow, perhaps magically, retards darkness. If you've only cut the avocado in half, close it back up around the pit. If the meat is in a bowl, put the pit in the bowl and push the meat around it (and cover with plastic wrap if it has to sit for any length of time).

A less magical but just as effective method is to sprinkle lemon or lime juice on the exposed flesh, or to cover it with a layer of butter, margarine, or mayonnaise.

Difficult to peel: There is no easy way to peel an avocado, but many avocados are peeled unnecessarily. There is often no need, despite what recipes may tell you. Do this instead: Cut it in half lengthwise and separate the two halves. Wham the blade (not the point) of a big knife into the pit, twist it slightly, and the pit will lift neatly out. Now you can scoop the meat out with a spoon or, for variety in salads, with a melon baller.

Not enough: In a salad, avocado combines well with citrus fruit sections. In a tossed salad, don't worry. No one will notice. In a dip, fill it out with cream cheese softened with milk to avocado consistency. When mixed in well and seasoned again, it will never show. If you're still worried, add a drop or two of green food coloring.

Too hard: If you are sick of avocado salads, consider using the firm ones as an ingredient in casseroles or crepe fillings, especially ones that include chicken or shrimp. Or how about a gourmet burrito with thin slices of avocado in the filling?

Too many: If you are sick of guacamole, whole avocados can be stored in the refrigerator. They won't ripen (or overripen) as fast. To preserve the appearance and increase the longevity of sliced avocados, coat the exposed parts with butter, margarine, or mayonnaise. Then you can keep them for days in the refrigerator. The thicker you smear the fat on, the longer it is likely to preserve the flesh.

Uncertain quality: Press the avocado with your thumb. If it dents easily, it is ready to use. If the grocer complains, tell him we said it was all right. If you've cut it open and wonder if the darker stained-looking portions are safe to eat—they are, but you'll probably want to mask them with an opaque dressing such as mayonnaise (or make guacamole, after all).

Unripe: Seal the avocado in a brown paper bag and keep it in a warm, but not hot, place. If the avocado has already been cut open and found to be unripe, you can still coat the exposed surfaces (with butter or margarine—but not mayonnaise, please, because it will go bad too quickly) and close the avocado up around the pit. Put it in the paper bag and check it the next day.

B

BACON

Curling: Once bacon is already fairly curly, the only thing to do is to put something heavy and flat on it—like a pot full of water—right on the griddle or in the frying pan. If it is already cooked and hopelessly curly, why not break it into small pieces and drop it into the eggs or whatever.

If bacon is just beginning to curl, dust the top lightly with flour, and the curling should be retarded.

Next time, bake the bacon at 400° for 10 to 15 minutes, instead of grilling or broiling it. If you bake it on a rack (or on your broiler pan in the oven) it'll be crispy and lovely. Baked bacon tastes just the same, but it just lies there, flat as a pancake. If you do wish to broil it, prick each slice in three or four places with a fork. It should lie flat.

On fire: Small fire? Drop a pot or pan on top of it to snuff it out. Big fire? Pour on baking soda or salt. Lots.

Stuck together: Method 1: Roll the entire package up crosswise. Unroll, and unless the pigs were fed on a diet of glue, all the bacon strips should be unstuck. Method 2: Drop the whole stuck-together bundle onto the griddle, under the broiler, or in the oven. It will come unstuck as it cooks and the melting fat acts as a lubricant. You can separate the slices and spread them out one at a time.

BAKED BEANS: *see* BEANS, BAKED

BAKING POWDER

Have none, need some: For every cup of flour in the recipe, mix 2 teaspoons of cream of tartar, 1 teaspoon of bicarbonate of soda, and ½ teaspoon of salt. Use this right away; it won't be effective for more than a day or so.

If your recipe happens to use buttermilk or sour milk, you can add ¼ teaspoon of baking soda to each ½ cup of milk in the recipe.

Uncertain quality: Stale baking powder can ruin whatever you're making. But old powder isn't necessarily stale. Here is a simple test for baking powder staleness: Put 1 teaspoonful in a cup of hot water. If it bubbles a lot, it's good. If it doesn't, throw it out.

BANANAS

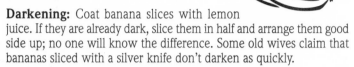

Bland: Sprinkle sliced bananas with, spices, for example, anise, cinnamon, or nutmeg.

Darkening: Coat banana slices with lemon juice. If they are already dark, slice them in half and arrange them good side up; no one will know the difference. Some old wives claim that bananas sliced with a silver knife don't darken as quickly.

Not enough: You'll have to fill out with something. Ripe pears go well with bananas without imposing too much on the flavor or smoothness. In a salad, try a cantaloupe to keep a lonely banana company; the colors are lovely together and the taste isn't bad, either.

Overripe, mushy: Here are two very simple and good things made from overripe or mushy bananas:

BANANA EGGNOG À LA MARIAH

1 mushy banana
1 cup cold milk
**1 egg (dipped for 1 minute in boiling water, so you
    don't get salmonella)**
Dash of salt

Blend together. Drink. Want to turn it into a treat? Add a scoop of your favorite frozen dairy dessert before blending and sprinkle cinnamon or nutmeg on top before serving.

SUSANNAH'S ROAST BANANAS

Remove one thin strip of peel. Brush the exposed banana with butter. Roast in a 400° oven or over coals until the entire peel is black. Eat directly from the peel with a spoon.

Too many (and they're all ripe at once): Well, you'll just have to make a banana cream pie. This can be absurdly simple if you use a store-bought pie shell, canned or dairy-case vanilla pudding, and spray-on whipped topping. See your favorite cookbook for homemade alternatives.

What, you still have more? All right. Mash them up, combine the bananas with lemon juice (1 lemon for each 6 bananas; or you can use that citric acid stuff groceries sell for home fruit processing) and *freeze* them in an airtight container or in freezer wrap. See, Chiquita, you *can* put bananas in the refrigerator, yes yes yes yes. Now you have six months to find some interesting recipes for mashed bananas—banana bread, banana cake, and banana pudding for starters. Thaw fully before unwrapping or opening, or the banana will turn brown. (Although if it does, the taste is unimpaired.)

OR

(For some readers, this hint alone is worth the price of the book.) Why not experiment with the latest in low-fat or fat-free baking? Many cake, cookie, and muffin recipes can be adapted to eliminate from ¾ to all the fat by substituting fruit purées (like applesauce or mashed bananas). Chocolate things work really well with bananas. Use one egg white for each whole egg in the recipe, and you're really creating a healthier version of your goodie, without those mysterious ingredients in the commercially available baked goods. It may take a little experimenting to get the proportions just right (start by using ¾ as much mashed banana as butter or fat in the recipe—add more if it's too dry), but you'll be doing yourself a lot of good!

BEANS, BAKED

Bland: Stir in some ketchup or chile sauce or Tabasco sauce or brown sugar or rosemary or (what the heck) all of them.

Burned: See Appendix A, regarding burned foods.

Not enough: Combine them with lima beans or kidney beans. Add brown sugar, or molasses and sugar, or maple syrup to make them taste more beany.

Salty: If they're very salty, about all you can do is add more beans (but not more salt, for goodness sake). If just slightly salty, a little brown sugar and/or a little vinegar will tend to override the salty flavor.

Time is short: Beans for baking should soak overnight. If you don't have time to do that, do this: Add 1 teaspoon of baking powder to 1 pound or so of beans, cover them with water, and cook at medium heat until they are soft, but not mushy—about 40 minutes. Add more water, if necessary, while they cook. Then drain off the water and bake as usual.

Uncertain quality: Dump the raw beans in water. The good ones will sink and the bad ones will float. Just as in real life.

BEANS, LIMA AND STRING

The two kinds of beans are combined because most of the problems facing the bean world are shared by these two.

Bland: A pinch of sugar in the cooking water helps bring out the flavor. On the plate or in the pot, try adding dill seed, fennel, or rosemary. Sage perks up Lima beans (⅛ teaspoon in the cooking water for a cup of dried beans), and sesame seed, sprinkled on string beans, is interesting. Toasted, slivered almonds make string beans downright elegant.

Frozen to the box: Run cold water into the spaces in the box, and the beans will come out.

Losing color: When beans start losing color, and when it is very important to you that they don't, then you may add a pinch of baking soda to the water. It will help them retain their color, but it will also extract most of the vitamins.

Not enough: In every San Francisco Italian restaurant, of which there are at least 750 excellent ones, you find something called Italian vegetables. Usually, but not always, this is a mixture of Italian beans, peas, and string beans. Very good. If you're desperate, even kidney or navy beans or chopped broccoli will do. Add a chunk of butter and cook together for 5 minutes so the flavors blend.

Old: If your string beans or Lima beans have been around for a week or more, add a pinch of sugar and ¼ teaspoon of salt to the cooking water.

Stringy: If your lima beans are stringy, you have more problems than this book can help you with. For stringy string beans, plunge them into boiling water for 3 minutes. Drain the water. They should be much easier to de-string.

Thawed: See Appendix B for a comment and a suggestion for frozen beans that have thawed before you wanted them to.

Too many: Lima beans reheat beautifully, especially if you brown ½ cup of minced onions and add them to the pot with a few tablespoons of water when reheating. Crumbled bacon on top is a nice touch. Just don't worry about Lima beans.

String beans make excellent salad material, when cold. Before putting them into the refrigerator, dress them with a mixture of 3 parts oil to 1 part lemon juice or vinegar. Salt and pepper to taste, and if you have some dill, add a couple of pinches. No dill? How about a dill pickle? Chop it fine and add it to the beans. (Remember that the pickle will add salt, so be careful in that department.)

BEAN SOUP: *see* **SOUPS**

BEEF: *see specific kinds of beef in the following categories:* **CHIPPED BEEF; CORNED BEEF; HAMBURGERS; LIVER; MEAT LOAF; POT ROAST; ROAST BEEF; STEAK; STEW.**

BEETS

Bland: Add a pinch of ground cloves or allspice to the cooking water—or chervil (about ¼ teaspoon per serving). Or sprinkle the cooked beets with dill weed or mustard seed. Experiment with other seasonings. Beets are very adaptable.

Difficult to peel: Beets virtually peel themselves if you treat them right. Put them in water, leaving about ½ inch of stem and root on them. Boil for 15 minutes. Then put them under cold running water. Cut off both ends, and the peel should slip right off.

Discoloring: Add 1 tablespoon of lemon juice or vinegar to the cooking water. Next time, do this at the start, just in case. It can do no harm.

Frozen to the box: Run some cold tap water into the carton, and the beets should unstick themselves forthwith.

Not enough: Beets and beet greens are a good combination. Cook the beet greens separately and mix them with cooked, diced beets. (Spinach, mustard, or other greens will do as well; in a pinch, so will lettuce leaves.) Add 1 tablespoon of vinegar and 1 teaspoon of sugar. If you are a bacon-fat saver, now's your chance. Add a scant tablespoon to the cooking water for a Southern flavor.

Another possibility is to grate raw beets, using the smallest holes on your grater. Pile the grated beets onto lettuce leaves. Add a small quantity of vinaigrette dressing to flavor.

Old: Add a pinch of sugar and a pinch of salt for each cup of liquid you're cooking the beets in. The former sweetens them back to their natural sweetness; the latter helps retain color and flavor.

Salty: If pickled beets are too salty, soak them in clear water for 10 minutes and store them in new water. If cooked beets are too salty, drain the water, replace with non-salty water, add a dash of either sugar or vinegar—or both—and cook a few more minutes.

Too many: Of course you can always pickle them (see how under **BEANS, LIMA AND STRING, Too many**, and omit the dill). Or, better yet, surprise everyone tomorrow with this easy borscht:

TATIANA'S BORSCHT

1 package dehydrated vegetable soup
1 pound beef-stew-type beef, cut in small pieces
Leftover beets
2 teaspoons dill weed, or ½ teaspoon fresh dill,
or 1 teaspoon dill seed
Dollops of sour cream
1 boiled potato per person

Make the vegetable soup using twice the amount of water called for. Simmer the beef in the soup for 1½ to 2 hours, or until it is very tender. Add the beets and dill, and cook 10 minutes more. Serve with sour cream on top. A boiled potato in each bowl makes this a whole meal.

BEET GREENS: *see* GREENS

BERRIES

Bland: Sprinkle them with brown sugar, confectioners' sugar, or one of the slightly sweet seasonings, such as nutmeg, cinnamon, or anise seed. If there is some juice, drop a whole cardamom or two into it during storage.

Frozen to the box: Run cold tap water into the box, and the berries will detach themselves almost at once.

Leafy, twiggy: Some times there are lots of little leaves and twigs mixed in with the berries, especially if you've picked them yourself. The fastest way to deleaf and detwig a large pail of berries is to pour them from one container to another across the path of an electric fan or a vacuum cleaner hose fastened to the blowing instead of the sucking nozzle. Please aim the air in the right direction. Otherwise see a good first-aid text on removing berry twigs from the ear.

Not enough: In a pie, use your emergency vanilla pudding and make it a berry cream pie. Either use the berries and the pudding in layers, or mix them together. Top with a meringue, and everyone will think that was what you planned all along.

For a shortcake, combine berries with fresh peaches, nectarines, or even pears. If you use pears, mix them with a sauce made from ¼ cup of water, 2 tablespoons of sugar, and ¼ teaspoon of almond extract, to give them more flavor.

Overripe: Make fruit sauce. Clean the berries as well as you can, eliminating all the fuzzy ones. Mash the rest with sugar to taste (start with 1 tablespoon per cup of berries) and serve with ice cream or shortcake or cream or all three.

Or use them in a deep-dish pie or a cobbler. Overripe berries are very juicy, but this won't matter as you have only a top crust.

Sour: Stir them with sugar and allow them to stand at room temperature for at least an hour. Use about 1 tablespoon of sugar per cup of berries.

Thawed: See Appendix B, regarding frozen foods that have thawed out too soon.

Too many: Clean the berries and spread them out one layer deep on a cookie sheet. Freeze until firm, and pour them into some sort of storage container; freezer bags do nicely. Then when berries are out of season, you will have the equivalent of fresh ones and not the sugar-soaked kind you usually have to settle for.

Another alternative is to make jelly or jam. Consult any good cookbook for directions. Making jam isn't nearly as hard as most people think it is.

Wet: Nobody likes a wet berry. Line a big tray or cookie sheet with paper towels. Pour the berries on it. Pat them gently with more paper towels.

BISCUITS: *see* BREAD AND ROLLS; MUFFINS

BLACKBERRIES: *see* BERRIES

BLUEBERRIES: *see* BERRIES

BOILED BEEF: *see* CORNED BEEF

BOUILLON: *see* SOUPS

BOYSENBERRIES: *see* BERRIES

BRANDY: *see* ALCOHOL

BREAD AND ROLLS: *see also* CAKE; COOKIES; MUFFINS; PIES

Bland: Once it's made, you can't make the bread more interesting, so put interesting things on it. For the breadbasket at dinner, try making interesting-flavored butters. Cream butter with herbs, spices, grated onion, or crushed garlic. If you're serving fish or poultry, try creaming orange or lemon zest into the butter. Serve the flavored butter in an attractive crock or small bowl.

If you have some really good olive oil on hand, consider serving that instead of butter, as many trendy Italian restaurants do. Either serve each guest a small bowl of olive oil to dip the bread into, or provide a carafe of oil so each person can create a small pool of oil on a bread-and-butter (now a bread-and-olive-oil) plate for dipping.

If what you've got is bland sliced bread, toast it lightly and apply any of the above butters (and perhaps a flurry of sweet paprika). Cut the slices into strips, three to a slice, and serve it in a basket. They'll know you tried.

Next time, sprinkle on anise or toasted poppy seeds or sesame seeds before baking. Or sift some sage (1 tablespoon per loaf) or poultry seasoning in with the flour. If the main course is ham or pork, try adding ½ teaspoon cinnamon and 1 teaspoon of sugar per loaf to the bread dough.

Burned: If you are baking or heating bread and it burns slightly, you can remove the burned spots with an ordinary kitchen grater. If there are lots of burned spots, you can cut them off and patch up the scars with bread ointment. Bread ointment is simply a well-beaten egg. Brush it on the wounds with a pastry brush and keep on heating the bread.

Cold: There are two ways to make cold bread hot without cooking it any more. For crusty kinds of bread and rolls, dip them very briefly in a bowl of hot water and toss them into a 350° oven until they are as hot as you'd like. For softer breads and muffins, wrap them rather loosely in foil and heat for 5 minutes at 450°.

Difficult to slice: Heat the knife.

To slice soft bread very thin, about the only thing to do is to freeze it, slice, and defrost it.

Dough doesn't rise: When bread dough fails to rise, additional gentle heat often helps. If you have an electric heating pad, set it on low, put foil on the pad, and put the bowl of dough on the foil.

Another way to produce gentle heat is to put the bowl in the dish-washer and set it for just the drying cycle. (If you make a mistake here, see **BREAD AND ROLLS, Soggy.**)

Or put the bowl in your gas oven; the warmth from the pilot light may be enough. (Not all gas ovens have permanently-on pilot lights, how-ever.) Or put it in any oven (not turned on) over a large pan of boil-ing-hot water (a broiler-pan-full will do nicely).

Alternatively, mix more yeast into ¼ cup of warm water or milk. Let it stand 5 minutes; knead it into the dough, which should now rise. (see, however, **YEAST, Expired.**)

Sometimes the second rising just doesn't come through, and you end up with a small, dense, loaf. Slice it very thin and see if it's accept-able as bread. If not, make bread crumbs or small croutons out of it and make new bread using new yeast.

Dough resists shaping: If it becomes unmanageable and doesn't "hang together," let it rest for 5 to 10 minutes, covered with a dampened cloth, while the gluten in the flour becomes elastic once again.

Dried out: Wrap the bread or rolls in a damp towel and refrigerate them for 24 hours. Then remove the towel and heat the bread in the oven at 350° for 5 minutes. It should be restored to something close to its normal condition.

Soggy: If sandwiches are needed and the bread is soggy, go ahead and make the sandwiches anyway, then grill the whole works briefly under the broiler. Unless you're given to making ice cream sand-wiches on bread, it shouldn't hurt the ingredients.

Stale: Here are two fast techniques that often help revitalize stale bread:

1. Pour ½ teaspoon of water on the bread, seal it up in a brown paper bag, and heat it in a 350° oven for 10 to 15 minutes.

2. Plunge the entire loaf (or rolls) into cold water for just an instant; then bake on a cookie sheet at 350° for 10 minutes.

Small amounts of very stale bread can, of course, be used to make bread crumbs, in your food processor or blender. If a whole loaf should go stale on you, make a classic American dessert. Here is a basic recipe. It is highly adaptable.

BEARS' BREAD PUDDING

3 to 5 cups stale bread (remove crust and dice
    the bread)
3 to 4 cups warm milk
$1/4$ teaspoon salt
3 to 4 eggs
$1/2$ to $3/4$ cup sugar, white or brown
$1/2$ cup confectioners' sugar (if you want this
    meringue-topped)
1 teaspoon vanilla

FLAVORING

$1/2$ teaspoon cinnamon plus $1/2$ teaspoon cloves
    (alternatively you can use $1/2$ teaspoon nutmeg)
Zest of 1 lemon
Juice of $1/2$ lemon

ADDITIONAL OPTIONS

$1/2$ cup raisins, dates, dried cranberries, nuts, or any
    combination of these
$1/2$ cup drained crushed pineapple
$1/4$ to $1/2$ cup orange marmalade or your favorite jam
1 to 2 tablespoons sherry or brandy (optional)

Put the bread into a baking dish. Combine milk and salt and
pour over the bread. Soak for 15 minutes. Separate the eggs.
Combine the yolks, white or brown sugar, flavoring and
optional ingredients of your choice. Mix well. Pour over the
soaked bread and use a fork to mix lightly. If you don't want
to bother with a meringue topping, whip the egg whites
until stiff and fold them into the mix. Set the pan in a
larger pan of hot water (this is a kind of custard) and bake
in a 350° oven for 45 minutes to 1 hour (how big is this
thing? How deep is your baking pan? It should be set but
not dried out when done.) Take it out to cool. To make a
meringue topping, turn the oven to 300°. Whip the egg
whites until foamy and add 2 tablespoons of confectioners'
sugar per egg white, continuing to beat. Add a good pinch
of cream of tartar, if you have it, and $1/2$ teaspoon of vanilla.
Pile it onto the pudding about 15 minutes before you want
to serve it and bake. (No need to put it in the water bath
this time.)

Stuck to pan: If bread sticks to whatever you're cooking or heating it in, wrap the whole works (bread and pan) in a dry towel while it is still hot. Let it sit outside the oven for 5 minutes. Unwrap, and presto!

Stuck to rolling pin: If bread dough sticks to the rolling pin and you don't want to add more flour by flouring the rolling pin, put the rolling pin in the freezer until it is very cold, and then roll out the dough.

BREADING

Falls off: This time, unless it came off in big replaceable slices, cover the whole works with a nontransparent sauce.

Next time, follow this six-step procedure: 1. Dry the object to be breaded. 2. Dip it in flour and shake off the excess, so there is only a thin coating. 3. Dip it in a mixture of an egg and a few drops of oil beaten well together. 4. Drop onto fine crumbs, to coat with a thin layer. (Spoon crumbs onto any bare spots and pat them on.) 5. Put on waxed paper in the refrigerator for 30 to 60 minutes. 6. Cook per recipe.

Note: Breaded objects reheated in a microwave oven become soggy. Reheat such things in a regular oven, please.

BROCCOLI

Bland: Mustard seed does interesting things to broccoli—either in the cooking water or sprinkled lightly over the finished product. A combination of tamari soy sauce and toasted sesame seeds will enliven either hot or cooked-and-chilled broccoli.

Frozen to the box: Run cold tap water into the box. The broccoli will come up for air promptly.

Not enough: A little hollandaise sauce will help. Everyone knows hollandaise is terribly rich, so they'll want less.

Or chop the broccoli up and combine it with cream of chicken soup or pea soup. Sprinkle with Parmesan cheese, paprika, and croutons, and you've either got a soup course—if it's thin—or an interesting side dish, depending on the amount of broccoli you started out with.

Old: When you cook old broccoli, add a pinch of sugar and a pinch of salt to each cup of cooking water.

Overcooked: If you have an awful lot of mushy broccoli, see the recipe for overcooked asparagus. You may then prefer to call the dish Timbale de Broccoli. Or you may call it anything you wish. There are those of us who think that naming dishes can be one of the enjoyable things about cooking.

Salty: If you've put too much salt in the cooking pot, first change the water; then rinse off the broccoli gently under hot water, holding it in a sieve or colander, and return it to the pot.

If broccoli on the plate is oversalted, wash it off the same way in very hot water. A little lemon juice, tossed gently with the broccoli, tends to freshen the taste.

Smelly: Is your broccoli smelling up the house as it cooks? Toss a heel of bread or a hot red pepper into the pot. Remove before serving.

Thawed: Please turn to Appendix B for one person's opinion of what to do when frozen food is prematurely thawed out.

Too much: Cooked broccoli will keep well for 5 days or so in the refrigerator. As soon as you're ready, you can make the following recipe:

BROCCOLI MAX

3 eggs
¹/₂ cup milk
1¹/₂ cups shredded Cheddar cheese
Dash of nutmeg
Pinch of pepper
Lots of broccoli

Mix all the nonbroccoli ingredients together. (You can tell which ones they are, because they aren't green.) Lay the broccoli in a baking dish (the quantity really isn't important). Pour the mixture over the broccoli, and bake it in a 350° oven for 30 minutes. Since what you are really doing is making a sort of broccoli custard, it is wise to rest the baking dish inside a larger dish or pan with about an inch of water on the bottom.

BROTH: *see* **SOUPS**

BROWN SUGAR: *see* **SUGAR**

BROWNIES: *see* **CAKE**

BRUSSELS SPROUTS

Everything said about broccoli, with the exception of **Overcooked**, applies equally well to Brussels sprouts. Please do not attempt to make Timbale de Brussels Sprouts.

Falling apart: Remove the loose outer leaves and mark an X on the stalk end of each sprout (that is, the place where it was attached to the Brussels sprout tree, or however they grow) with a sharp knife before cooking. This will help it all cook uniformly and be less likely to fall apart before it's done.

Overcooked: Like building a perpetual-motion machine and trisecting the angle, devising a recipe for overcooked Brussels sprouts had long been thought to be impossible. We have finally cracked the O.B.S. (Overcooked Brussels Sprouts) barrier!

OVERCOOKED BRUSSELS SPROUTS RECIPE

Overcooked Brussels sprouts
1 tablespoon oil
1 tablespoons vinegar (balsamic vinegar is
    especially nice here)
1 tablespoon brown (or white) sugar
1 tablespoon soy sauce (or $\frac{1}{4}$ teaspoon salt)
$\frac{1}{2}$ cup soft bread crumbs
$\frac{1}{4}$ cup grated Parmesan cheese

Drain the overcooked little devils as gently and thoroughly as possible. Meanwhile, combine the oil, vinegar, sugar, and soy sauce in a small saucepan and bring to a boil. Put a layer of soft bread crumbs, about $\frac{1}{2}$ inch thick, in the bottom of a baking dish. Lay the sprouts out on the crumbs. Pour the sauce on them, and cover with a flurry of more crumbs and the Parmesan cheese. You should warm this in the oven at 350°, but since it's already overcooked, don't wait too long.

BUTTER

Burning (while sautéing or frying): Add a tiny bit of any kind of oil (except motor oil) to the butter when you see it is browning too fast. It doesn't change the flavor, and oil plus butter doesn't burn as easily as butter alone. Badly burned butter does have a distinctive taste, so if you have enough extra butter, why not start over? If you don't pour off the melted butter, mix with a little oil, put it back in the pan, and hope for the best.

Have none, need some: In baking, you can substitute 1 cup plus 2 tablespoons of Crisco or comparable product for 1 cup of butter. If a buttery flavor is required, add a few drops of butter flavoring. Of course, no one has butter flavoring on hand, so when you send someone out to get some, you might ask them to pick up a pound or two of butter. . . .

Another approach entirely is the one detailed under **BANANAS, Too many**. If you're interested in low-fat cookery, it's worth considering.

For purposes other than baking, see the useful suggestion under **WHIPPED CREAM, Overwhipped, separated**.

Too hard to cream: Shred the butter with either a grater or a potato peeler for a smallish amount. If you've got lots of butter to cream, you can grate it with the grating disk of your food processor. In any case, warm the bowl you're going to be creaming in to help the process (hold the bowl upside down over the sink and run hot water on the outside). If you're using sugar in your recipe, try heating the sugar before adding it to the butter.

Alternatively, you can soften butter almost instantly in a microwave. Heat an unwrapped cube of butter for 10 seconds on medium setting and then let it stand for 5 minutes.

Too hard to spread: The problem is how to soften the butter without melting it. The solution is to cover the butter with a hot bowl for a few minutes, or to microwave it on the lowest setting for 1 minute and then let it stand for 5 minutes. If this is a frequent problem, check your local kitchen-supply store or mail-order catalog for a British butter dish—a terra-cotta outer dish that is soaked daily in cold water. The butter stays cool and spreadable in an inner glass dish.

BUTTERMILK

Have none, need some: In many recipes, you can substitute ¼ cup milk plus ¾ cup yogurt for 1 cup of buttermilk.

CABBAGE

Bland: Try adding any or all of the following three seeds to the cooking water: dill, mustard, and sesame.

Discoloring: Red cabbage sometimes turns purple or blue during cooking. Add 1 tablespoon of vinegar to the cooking water, and it will turn red again.

Not enough: Cold cabbage (slaws and salads) fills out well with lettuce, shredded carrots, and diced celery, and combines beautifully with pineapple (top with chopped nuts), apples (dice with the peel on, and add some horseradish to the dressing—start with 1 teaspoon and taste), and pears (add 1 teaspoon of curry powder for each cup of pears to the dressing and top with a small mound of plumped raisins).

Hot cabbage can be sliced up into smaller pieces (assuming it was in wedges) and put into a baking dish. This is a messy job, but don't worry; it will come out looking all right. Pour cheese sauce or melted cheese over it all. Run it under the broiler until it just begins to brown. Have any bacon crumbles? Too bad; all right, decorate with nuts (such as toasted almonds), sliced olives, or good old paprika. Perhaps a shake or two of caraway seeds.

If you have tomatoes on hand, you might consider making:

CABBAGE RANCHERO

The quantities for this recipe are extremely variable, depending on how far you want to stretch your cabbage.

Cabbage (cooked, cut into small pieces or chunks)
Onions (fresh and chopped, or dehydrated)
Butter
Tomatoes
Ketchup
Chile powder

Brown the onions in butter. Chop tomatoes and add to the onions. Cook about 10 minutes, stirring occasionally. Toss in the cooked cabbage, add a few tablespoons of ketchup and a rounded teaspoon of chile powder and there you are.

Old: Add a pinch of salt to each cup of the cooking water. This will help elderly cabbage retain, during the cooking, what flavor it has left.

Overcooked: Make cabbage soup (see **CABBAGE, Too much**, for directions).

Alternatively, drain the cabbage very well by patting in paper towels after draining in a colander. If it survives this treatment, it is probably edible as is. Season it with garlic salt and pepper; toss with butter in a warmed bowl, if you do that sort of thing.

Smelly: The old-wives' remedy to prevent cabbage from stinking up the entire block is to put a piece of bread, especially a thick slice from the end of the loaf, in the pot along with the cabbage. Rye bread seems to work the best, but any sort will have some effect in this antipollution campaign.

If the cabbage smell is already everywhere in the house, there is a good way to overcome it, if you like the smell of cloves. The odor of cloves tends to blot out the odor of cabbage. Produce eau de clove by simmering three or four whole cloves in a pan with vinegar in it. If you then decide that the cloves smell worse than the cabbage, you're out of luck.

Too much: For raw cabbage, wrap it well in plastic wrap or aluminum foil. It will keep a week if it is fresh. So worry about it next Thursday.

For cooked cabbage, chop it up and refrigerate it. Tomorrow, make:

CABBAGE-CHICKEN POTAGE FELIPE

Cooked cabbage
1 can cream of chicken soup
1 can's worth of milk
1 slice of rye bread per person
or
Caraway seeds
1 slice of any other bread per person
Butter
Shredded cheese and/or toasted almonds

Combine the cooked cabbage with the can of soup diluted with the milk. If you're using them, add the caraway seeds (start with 1 tablespoon and see how you think it looks). Toast and butter the bread and put one slice in each soup bowl. Pour hot soup over the bread and let it stand 3 minutes to soak the rye. Top with a healthy pinch of cheese or almonds.

CAKE: *see also* BREAD AND ROLLS; COOKIES; CREAM PUFFS; ICING; MUFFINS

Bubbles in the batter: Put the batter in the pan. Hold the pan about 6 inches above the floor. Drop it. Do this three or four times, or until the people from downstairs come up to complain, whichever occurs first. The bubbles will go away and so, if you are lucky, will the people from downstairs.

Burned: If the cake is fully cooked, either cut away the burned parts and cover the cake with icing (even if you hadn't intended to), or use a steel grate to "file" away the burned spots. If the cake's too small now, slice it into layers and consider using a liqueur to sprinkle on the slices. Sandwich it back together with filling or frosting.

If the cake is not fully cooked but the top is too brown, cut away the browned parts and cover the wounds with a first-aid dressing made from a beaten egg mixed with 1 teaspoon of brown sugar. Brush it on with a pastry brush and continue baking (lower the oven temperature by 25°).

Cooking unevenly: If you check your cake while it is cooking (and you should, after 15 or 20 minutes) and the edges look done while the center is soggy, lower the temperature by 50°. You may need to increase the baking time. Check again in 15 or 20 minutes (and later, check your oven control against an oven thermometer; it may be off).

Crumbly; can't ice it or slice it: Freeze it, Ice it. Slice it. Thaw it. Go, team, go!

Drying out: If you intend to use the cake fairly soon, brush some melted butter on the top and sides. This retards drying and also makes it easier to spread the icing on. If the cake is drying out in storage, put something moist in with the cake, underneath the cake cover. The cover should be as airtight as possible. The moistest thing of all is a small glass of water. A slice of apple or orange will do nicely, too. Don't forget to add water or change slices every 2 or 3 days.

Remember, too, that most cakes can be successfully frozen.

Flat, soggy, fallen: If your cake is flat or soggy, you may have forgotten to put in the baking powder. No known remedial measure can correct this problem. (Forget the bicycle-pump idea. That only works in cartoons.) As Escoffier (or perhaps it was Joe at Le Greasy Spoon) said, "The cake shall never rise again."

But fallen cake still *tastes* pretty good, even if it looks dreadful. Use your imagination to come up with an interesting fallen-cake recipe. One example should suffice:

JESSIE'S APPLE MOOSH

Fallen cake
Applesauce (sweetened; canned or homemade)
Whipped cream

Break fallen cake into chunks. Mix with applesauce. Serve topped with whipped cream. No one will ever know it wasn't intentional. Is that too easy? Okay, you can:

- Spread jam on the cake before you break it up

- Sprinkle sherry or liqueur on before applying the whipped topping

- Plump raisins in hot water or warmed rum, drain, and mix in with the applesauce

Lopsided: Check your cake after 20 minutes of cooking. As a rule, if it is going to turn out lopsided because of a defective oven or a tilted kitchen or whatever, turning (the cake) halfway around halfway through the baking process should even it up. Check again after another 20 minutes. Keep turning, if necessary. If a finished cake is lopsided, slice the top even, and turn the cake upside down before frosting.

Stale: Unfortunately, there is no good way to unstale a cake. Fortunately, a lot of dessert recipes work very well, sometimes even better, with stale cake. Check your big cookbooks. We suggest two possibilities for stale cake, one chocolate and one vanilla:

JUDY'S CHOCOLATE MERINGUE MARVEL

Stale chocolate cake, cut into 1-inch cubes
Meringue made from 2 tablespoons of sugar for each egg white
Grated coconut or chopped pecans

Put cake cubes in a baking dish. Pile meringue on thickly. Sprinkle with coconut or pecans. Heat in a 300° oven until the meringue is browned.

VANILLA RUM DELIGHT

1 tablespoon rum for each cup of cake cubes
Stale white cake, cut into 1-inch cubes
Thick vanilla pudding
Whipped cream

Sprinkle rum onto cake. Mix into pudding. Chill. Serve with whipped cream.

Stuck to cellophane wrapper: Iced packaged cakes tend to stick to their wrappers. To avoid that nasty possibility, hold the package under the cold water faucet for about 20 to 30 seconds before unwrapping. (This works better if there is water coming out of the faucet.)

Stuck to pan: This is one of the most fertile areas for household hint thinker-uppers. Many techniques have been proposed, and they all have merit:

1. Let the cake sit for 5 minutes; it will shrink a little, and may be easier to remove.

2. Remove the pan from the oven and place it on a cloth that you have soaked in cold water and wrung out.

3. Loosen the edges with a knitting needle rather than a knife, place a wire rack on top, invert the whole works, and tap the bottom of the pan, if necessary, with a spoon.

4. Wrap the cake and pan in a towel as it comes out of the oven and let it stand for 5 minutes.

5. If the cake is cold and stuck, reheat it for a few minutes.

Next time, don't use salted butter to grease the pan; it makes things more likely to stick.

Stuck to rolling pin: Wait a minute—what are you doing rolling out cake dough? Well, if you must, chill the rolling pin in the freezer, and the dough won't stick.

Too soft; can't ice it or slice it: Freeze it. Ice it. Slice it. Thaw it. Rah, team, rah!

CANDY

Fudge (and other such) too hard: During cooking: add a little milk and cook to the proper temperature. After cooking: if the fudge won't pour, add 1 tablespoon of milk and 2 or 3 tablespoons of corn syrup;

beat until smooth and pour at once. After it has cooled: put it in an airtight container. The fudge should become softer and more velvety within 24 hours.

Fudge won't fudge: Fudge that won't fudge (fudge makers will know that feeling of beating a heavy, syrupy glop that just won't firm up) is most certainly not cooked enough. Scrape it back into the saucepan, add a teaspoon or two of water, and keep cooking, stirring constantly.

Divinity fudge cannot be made on humid days. If you've tried, and you have pools of sticky white stuff, scrape it into a bowl, beat in a few teaspoons of cream or milk, and use it as a great sauce on chocolate ice cream.

Stuck together: If hard candies stick together in the jar or bowl, separate them by hand (unless you have a machine for the purpose) and sprinkle them lightly with granulated (or, better yet, superfine granulated) sugar before returning them to the container. (You can convert regular granulated sugar into superfine in your food processor.)

Sugaring: When chocolate candies start sugaring while cooking, add a little bit of milk and keep cooking until the mixture returns to the prescribed temperature. Crystals tend to cause sugaring, which is why many confection recipes tell you to wash down the sides of your cooking pan with a pastry brush dipped in water a few times during a long cooking process.

CANS (KEY-OPENING TYPE)

Key is missing: Try using a regular can opener on the opposite side. Write a nasty letter to the manufacturer.

Key is stuck halfway through opening can: Holding the can with an oven mitt or a dishtowel, try sticking a table knife through the hole in the key handle to get more leverage. (If you use your naked hands, you may as well get the Band-Aids out first to save time.) If this fails, and the contents can't be scraped out, hold the can over a bowl and use a can opener on the other side. Write a *very* nasty letter to the manufacturer.

Many cans that used to be key-opening (like those containing anchovies) are now pull-tab opening. They still get stuck halfway along. You can improve your leverage with two thick pads of paper towel (or two kitchen towels). Hold the opened end down with one protected hand and grab the whole pull-top with the other. Growl loudly and pull. Apologize if you scared the cat.

CARROTS

Bland: Try adding any of the following seasonings to cooked carrots: roughly ¼ teaspoon per four servings of ground cloves, ginger, mace, marjoram, poppy seed, or thyme. Consider ketchup or chile sauce over cooked carrots.

Burned: See Appendix A regarding burned foods.

Not enough: For raw carrots, use with any other raw vegetable on a relish plate. Or shave them with a vegetable peeler, and sink the peelings in a huge bowl of ice water. They will curl up, and when you have drained off the water, will look like three times as much.

For cooked carrots, cook them until soft and see the recipe for what to do with overcooked carrots. Or mix them with peas (say, there's an original idea!), broccoli plus cheese sauce, or Lima beans.

Old: How old are we talking here? A little shriveled or limp, but basically intact? For raw carrots, soak them in ice water overnight. Adding the juice of one lemon or a tablespoon of vinegar to the water can help bring back some life, but isn't essential. But face it, once any vegetable gets slimy it belongs in the compost heap.

For cooked carrots, add a pinch of sugar and ¼ teaspoon of salt to each cup of cooking water.

Overcooked: Try making the following:

ALEXA'S CARROT CASSEROLE

Overcooked carrots
Mashed potatoes (even instant ones)
Cheese of any kind

Mash carrots up with the potatoes. Pile into a casserole, top with the cheese, and put under the broiler until the cheese melts.

See also the soup suggestions under **ASPARAGUS, Overcooked**.

Thawed: See Appendix B regarding foods that have been thawed out before you wish to use them.

Too many: Aw, come on. Carrots keep almost a month when wrapped well in plastic wrap or foil. You're bound to think of something in thirty days. If they're already peeled, however, consider making a dip to dunk them in for an appetizer. Or make a carrot salad for tomorrow's dinner. You're having carrot salad *today*? Then cook them and see the next paragraph.

With a surplus of cooked carrots, consider the following:

DILLY CARROTS

4 cups cooked carrots
1 teaspoon dill seed, or weed, or ³/₄ teaspoon
chopped fresh dill
Dash of celery seed
Vinaigrette

Combine the herbs and vinaigrette. Toss with the carrots and marinate overnight, well covered. Keeps several days and just gets more dilly.

Are you feeling really experimental? Make this:

INDIAN CARROT PUDDING

Cooked carrots
¹/₄ cup butter for every 2 cups carrots
Cream or milk
1 tablespoon lime or lemon juice
2 heaping tablespoons chopped nuts (any kind)
2 tablespoons raisins
2 or more tablespoons sugar
¹/₈ teaspoon almond extract
Whipped cream

Drain the carrots well. Mash them with butter to reach mashed potato consistency. (Add a little cream or milk if necessary.) Add lime or lemon juice, nuts, and raisins. Sweeten until it tastes good to you. Add the almond extract, if you are so inclined. You can serve this hot or cold, topped with whipped cream, or even frozen vanilla yogurt or ice cream. Talk about pumpkins and squashes at dinner and see if anyone figures out what you really made the dessert from. (They won't.)

Wilted: *see* **CARROTS, Old.**

CATSUP: *see* SAUCES

CAULIFLOWER

Bland: Two seasonings that go interestingly with bland cauliflower are mace (sprinkle on a pinch) and poppy seed (scatter 1 to 2 teaspoons per head).

Burned: See Appendix A regarding burned foods.

Discoloring: If the cauliflower isn't as white as you'd like, you'll have to cook it in boiling water (rather than steaming it) this time. Add a dash of vinegar after the water boils. It will whiten.

Not enough: Cooked cauliflower is a strange-shaped (cauliflower-shaped, you might say) vegetable that doesn't really toss well with anything. But you can put any other vegetable (cooked) on the bottom of a greased baking dish, then a layer of cheese of any sort, then a layer of cauliflower, and a final sprinkling of cheese on the top. Use a tablespoon of the bottom vegetable as a garnish as fair warning to diners.

Old: Add a pinch of sugar and another pinch of salt to each and every cup of water you use in cooking it. They will help retain sweetness, flavor, and color.

Overcooked: Let us tell you about overcooked cauliflower. It is an absolute godsend to dieters. You know all those things people make with white sauce (casseroles, gravies, timbales, etc.)? You can make awfully good much-lower-fat facsimiles with overcooked cauliflower.

Keep cooking it until it is completely soft when you poke it with a spoon. Then mash it absolutely smooth (a blender or food processor will do this quickly). Add milk until you have the consistency of loose mashed potatoes.

Save this glop in the refrigerator to combine, for example, with defatted turkey drippings for lovely, guiltless, gravy. Quite good, too, on real mashed potatoes.

Or make:

DAVE'S MOCK POTATO PUFF

Overcooked cauliflower
Onion powder
Salt
Pepper
Parmesan cheese

Mash up the cauliflower, add the seasonings to taste, pour it into a baking dish, top with Parmesan cheese, and bake for half an hour at 350°.

Salty: If cauliflower is too salty on the plate, put it back in clean, new, boiling water for 1 minute. If you discover you've oversalted the cooking water, change it immediately.

Smelly: Many hold that most of the smells that emanate from a cooking cauliflower come from the water. And most of the smells enter the water during the first 5 minutes of boiling. The solution, therefore, is to change the water after the cauliflower has boiled for 5 minutes.

If it is too late for that, toss a piece of bread (preferably rye) into the pot. Or make a solution of 1 part vinegar to 3 parts water, dip a cloth in it, wring it out, and spread it over the top of the pot while the cauliflower cooks. Be careful not to let the cloth catch fire from the burner.

Thawed: See Appendix B if your frozen cauliflower defrosted itself when you weren't looking.

Too much: Raw cauliflower keeps a long time, if it's cold and dry. Cooked cauliflower can be used in salads the next day. Or cover it with plastic wrap and refrigerate for two or three days. Then make:

ANDY'S INDIAN CAULIFLOWER PASTA

Equal volume of cooked cauliflower chunks and cooked pasta—chunked shaped is best, such as fuselli, radiatore, or medium shells

Combine with a sauce made of:

Peanut butter, loosened with bouillon to a
gravy consistency
1/8 teaspoon cayenne pepper
1 teaspoon garam masala (great roasted Indian spice
you can buy ready-made or make yourself)

Warm in a 350° oven for 30 minutes. This works equally well
with broccoli. The peanut butter can be smooth or chunky.

CELERY

Bland: Raw celery is vastly improved by filling the trough with some
sort of delectable cheese goo like this one: caviar (red or black, cheap
or good) with sour cream or cream cheese, plus a bit of Roquefort
cheese. Soften it with milk if it is too stiff.

Cooked celery is perked up nicely if you add mustard or poppy seed
to the cooking water. (They cook celery? Sure. Consider it next time
you need another vegetable, on its own or to fill out a smaller amount
of something else.)

Old: *see* CELERY, Soggy

Soggy: Soak wilted celery stalks in ice water for 2 to 3 hours. Option:
Add 1 tablespoon of vinegar or the juice of one lemon. It is said to help
retain the flavor.

As an alternative, wash the celery, stand it vertically for 2 hours in a
pitcher of cold water plus 1 teaspoon of salt, in the refrigerator.

Here is one of the world's only recipes for hopelessly soggy celery:

SOGGY CELERY DISH

Hopelessly soggy celery
1 (11-ounce) can consommé
1/2 cup water
Vinaigrette

Poach old and hopelessly soggy celery in consommé plus
water for 10 minutes. Drain. Split the stalks in half the long
way. Cover them with vinaigrette dressing. Chill in the
refrigerator for at least 4 hours before serving.

CEREAL

Bland: Oh my goodness, everything under the sun can be stirred into or sprinkled onto hot or cold cereals to make them more interesting. Just for starters:

Make hot cereal using chocolate milk instead of regular milk.

Add 1 teaspoon of cinnamon, a dash of ginger, or a few cloves (tied in cheesecloth so you can remove them) to hot water before adding the cereal.

Stir a cup of canned chopped fruit (per 4 servings) into hot cereal halfway through the cooking process. Add prunes, dates, raisins, currants, nuts, or other dried fruits to hot or cold cereals.

Plump dried fruits in hot water and let stand 3 minutes for the fruit to rehydrate. Let cool before adding to cold cereal.

Put 1 tablespoon of jam in a bowl, add a bit of milk, mush them together, and add the cereal, hot or cold.

Put chocolate bits into oatmeal. (Think about chocolate chip oatmeal cookies.)

Are you really experimental? Here's a great camping breakfast for that morning when you can't face another bowl of oatmeal.

RICHARD'S LAYERED OATMEAL

Brown sugar
Oatmeal
Shredded cheddar cheese

Put a layer of brown sugar on the bottom of a bowl. Carefully pile on a thick layer of hot oatmeal. Top with a layer of shredded Cheddar cheese. If you can, cover the bowl with a plate or other solid cover and let it stand for a couple of minutes to let the cheese melt onto the oatmeal. You then eat the top savory layer first (if you like sharp Cheddar, this is especially good), and eat the bottom sweet layer as your dessert.

Eat cold cereal with eggnog or instant malted milk.

Sweeten cereals with brown sugar or maple sugar or maple syrup or fruit sundae syrup. Add ice cream, maraschino cherries, marshmallows, and/or vanilla extract.

Go really nuts. Serve a tossed salad with a bland dressing (such as a creamy French) and pour breakfast cereal (Kix, Cheerios, Chex) over it, like croutons.

Loose: For hot cereal, add more cereal. For cold cereal, what in the world can you mean by this?

Lumpy: Push hot lumpy cereal through a strainer. This will probably make it loose. (see **CEREAL, Loose.**) Next time, start with cold water and stir constantly, if you think it is worth the effort.

Soggy: Somebody left the cold cereal open on the muggiest day of the year and your cereal is limp and soggy. Pour it onto a cookie sheet and bake it for 2 or 3 minutes at 350°. When it cools, it should have re-crisped itself.

CHARD: see GREENS

CHEESE

Cooked cheese that is rubbery, tough, stringy: This happens when there is too much heat. The excessive heat separated the fat from the protein in the cheese and the result is a Welsh rarebit (or whatever) that is rubbery, tough, stringy, and often looks awful.

This time, dump the cheese in a blender or food processor and blend (at low speed in the blender) for a minute or so to break down the rubberiness. Pour it back into the pan or, better yet, into the top of a double boiler, and continue cooking. If the blending makes it too loose, add some browned flour (flour that you have browned on a baking sheet in a 400° oven) until it is the proper consistency.

Next time, cook the cheese from the start in the top of a double boiler, making sure the bottom of the top pot isn't touching the boiling water below. It'll take a little longer than using direct heat, but it's foolproof.

Dried out, stale: If it is extremely hard, grate it (any cheese can be grated) and use it as a topping for vegetables, eggs, or in soufflés.

If it is dry but not all that dry, slice off the crusty edges (you can grate those), and either coat the bare edges with melted butter or wrap the whole cheese in a cloth that has been soaked in vinegar and wrung out. (Do you suppose that's what cheesecloth is really for?) Store the cheese in the refrigerator, in any case.

Hard (difficult to cut): Slicing a large piece of firm cheese such as Cheddar is made easier if you wrap it in plastic and microwave it for 30 to 40 seconds on medium power (depending on the size of the piece).

Moldy: Cut off the moldy parts; the rest of the cheese won't be affected. To prevent mold from recurring, wrap the cheese tightly in plastic.

Note: Please do not try to remove the mold from Roquefort or blue cheese. It is supposed to be there. Thank you.

Oily: Wrap the oily cheese in paper towels; they will absorb much of the excess oil within 3 days or so. When the towels becomes too oily, change them.

Soft, difficult to cut: Heat the knife or go out and buy a cheese-cutting gadget (a thin wire in a frame) for a couple of bucks.

Too much supposed-to-be-moldy cheese: Combine leftover blue or Roquefort cheese with an equal amount (by weight) of sweet butter. Add a dollop of Cognac and store in a covered jar in the refrigerator. It lasts nearly forever and is a great hors d'oeuvre served on crackers.

CHERRIES

Bland: For pies especially, it is nice if the cherries really taste like cherries. Surprisingly enough, they do even more if you add a few drops of almond extract to them. This is primarily for canned cherries but works with fresh ones as well.

Pale: In cherry pie you want the cherries to be a nice bright red. If nature didn't do it, cheat just a little and add a few drop of red coloring to whatever you use as the thickening agent.

Pits: If you don't have a Tom Swift Steam-Powered Automatic Cherry Pitter, you can use a hairpin. Press the rounded top of the hairpin (a paper clip works, too) into the cherry at the stem end, then down and under the pit, and lift up. Pin and pit should emerge leaving the cherry virtually unharmed.

Too many: Maybe now is the time to discover cherry preserves. Cherries are just about the easiest fruit to handle and therefore a good beginning lesson in your self-taught course in canning or freezing. Just think about Cherries Jubilee or hot cherry cobbler in the middle of winter. Home-frozen cherries last up to a year—in other words, until the next cherry season. Consult any comprehensive cookbook for step-by-step instructions.

CHESTNUTS: *see* NUTS

CHICKEN: *see* POULTRY

CHICKEN LIVERS: *see* LIVER

CHIPPED BEEF

Not enough: Stretch it by adding shredded Cheddar cheese to creamed chipped beef and serving it over biscuits instead of toast.

Salty: Dunk it in boiling water for about 5 seconds. Rinse in gently running cold water.

CHOCOLATE AND COCOA

Have one, need the other: Substitute 3 tablespoons of cocoa plus 1 tablespoon of shortening for 1 square of unsweetened chocolate, or vice versa.

Grayed: The gray film (or streaks) that appears on chocolate is utterly harmless. It is caused by the chocolate being heated and cooled improperly, so the components separate slightly and a thin layer of cocoa butter "blooms" on the surface. You can melt grayed chocolate and use it as an ingredient, or just arrange to serve it in a darkened room.

Scum or skin on the surface of drinking cocoa: Remove it with a cold spoon; then float a marshmallow on the top to keep the skin from reappearing.

Stiffened up: Water droplets, high temperature, and quirks of the chocolate sometimes cause melting chocolate to go stiff in the pan. The best rescue remedy is a teaspoon of vegetable shortening stirred in. Add more, if needed, to bring the chocolate to the desired consistency. Butter, which contains some water, will not work as well.

Melting chocolate stuck to pan: There is nothing you can do about it now. Next time, grease the pan very lightly, or use a double boiler and melt the chocolate over (not touching) boiling water.

CHOCOLATE SAUCE: *see* SAUCES

CLAMS: *see also* MUSSELS

Can't open: There is a long and involved procedure used by purists. You may be blackballed from the Clam Fanciers League for the following, but it works nicely, thank you: Drop the clams four at a time into boiling water. After 15 seconds, remove the clams from the water and slip a knife in between the shells. The water relaxes the muscle that is holding them shut.

Sandy, gritty: Sprinkle the clams with lots of cornmeal. Then pour on enough water to cover them. Wait 3 hours. They will have expelled the sand and grit. Wouldn't you in a similar situation?

Uncertain quality: It is always safest to buy clams in the shell. Be suspicious of broken shells or ones that aren't tightly closed. If in doubt, dump clams into cold water and discard any that float.

COCOA: *see* CHOCOLATE AND COCOA

COCONUTS

Can't open: Method 1: Pierce the softest of the three or more "eyes" with an ice pick or skewer, drain out the "milk" and crack the shell with a hammer. Method 2: Bake the coconut for 20 minutes at 300°. By the end of this time, it will have cracked itself open, or a light tap on the noggin (of the coconut) will do the job.

Dried up: Put the coconut meat in a bowl, cover it with cow's milk, and refrigerate for 1 hour. Press the meat dry in a strainer. (The milk can then be used for drinking or cooking.)

If you have the time, put the coconut in an airtight container in the refrigerator with a slice of fresh bread for 3 days, at the end of which time you will have fresh coconut and stale bread.

Stale shredded coconut: Method 1: Soak it in cow's milk plus a dash of sugar for 3 minutes. Method 2: Hold it in a sieve over boiling water until it is as moist as you would like.

COFFEE

Cloudy: Add eggshells to the coffee while it is heating.

Not enough: Company's coming any minute, and you're nearly out of coffee. Make mocha, and you can serve six people with 2 cups of coffee. Here's how:

MOCHA

⅓ cup cocoa powder
3 cups warmed milk
2 cups coffee
¼ cup or more sugar to taste
Rum or brandy (optional)
Dash of cinnamon

Add the cocoa and warmed milk (be careful not to let it boil) to coffee. Sweeten to taste. A glug of rum or brandy and a flurry of cinnamon can turn a potential disaster into an occasion.

For after dinner, try Café Brûlot. Three cups of coffee will serve six people:

CAFÉ BRÛLOT

6 ounces brandy (or a mixture of rum and brandy)
6 cloves
6 teaspoons sugar
A few strips of orange peel
3 cups coffee

Drag out the chafing dish, or herd everybody into the kitchen; this is too spectacular to be missed. In the chafing dish, heat the brandy, cloves, sugar and orange peel. When it is nice and hot, ignite the vapors. Slowly add the 3 cups of coffee to the flaming mixture, stirring slowly as you do. Serve in your smallest cups; this is supposed to be a demitasse.

Overcooked: A tiny pinch of salt is said, by some, to take away the bitter taste of overcooked coffee.

Too hot: If you overheat coffee on a regular basis, why not keep a small bowl of frozen coffee cubes in the freezer?

COLESLAW: see CABBAGE

CONSOMMÉ: see SOUPS

COOKIES: *see also* CAKE; MUFFINS

Bland: After baking (and tasting) the cookies, try brushing with egg white (health warning: always cook your egg 1 minute before using the white, to defeat salmonella beasts that might make you sick) and small amounts of anise seed, cumin, cinnamon, ginger, or nutmeg. Or spread them with peanut butter and top with cake decorations or fancies. Or make sandwich cookies: use any kind of jam or fudge for a filling. Got any chocolate chips on hand? Melt them and spread on for filling. Or make:

ORANGE CREAM CHEESE FROSTING

3 ounces cream cheese
1 tablespoon orange juice
1 teaspoon vanilla extract
3 cups sifted powdered sugar

Combine orange juice and vanilla. Cream the cream cheese until it is soft. Add the sugar gradually, beating constantly. Spread on cookies.

Or brush the tops of bland cookies with one egg white (no need to cook this one—it's about to get broiled), beaten until foamy, with 1 tablespoon of good sweet sherry, and sprinkle with slivered almonds. Broil for 1 minute to set the nuts.

Or glue a flat chocolate wafer (a nonpareil) to the middle of the cookies with a dot of frosting, or by laying the chocolate wafers on the cookies and putting them (carefully) into a 400° oven for just a minute to let the wafers melt slightly and adhere themselves to the cookies.

Burned (or burning): Cookies made on brown (generally nonstick) cookie sheets and/or cookie sheets with sides are more likely to burn. Next time: use the flat and shiny ones.

If the sheet is half or less full of cookies, it may absorb too much heat and get too hot. Put an inverted baking pan on the empty half.

Crisp: Cookies that are too crisp will usually de-crisp themselves if stored in an airtight container for at least 24 hours.

Crumbly dough: If the cookie dough is too crumbly, but you don't want to add more moisture, try letting the dough stand at room temperature for half an hour, covered with a slightly dampened cloth.

Hard: Cookies that are hard will soften if stored in an airtight container with something from which they can absorb moisture. A glass of water does nicely; so does a slice or two of fresh bread.

Spreading problems: If cookie dough doesn't spread out satisfactorily before or during baking, take something cold and smooth and flatten out each cookie with a rotary motion. Suggested cold and smooth thing number 1: a spoon dipped in cold water. Suggested cold and smooth thing number 2: an ice cube wrapped in a smooth cloth or plastic wrap. If, however, it spreads too much, the problem may well be that the cookie sheet is too warm. For the next batch, turn the sheet over and run cold water on the back (no need to dry it). Then put the cookies to cook on the other side.

Stuck to cookie sheet: Run the sheet or tin over a hot burner on the range. Or wrap the whole works in a towel as it comes hot from the oven and let it stand for 5 minutes. Sometimes greasing the spatula helps.

Stuck to hands: Wash your hands in cold water. Or juggle a handful of ice cubes for as long as you can bear it. The dough won't stick.

Stuck to rolling pin: If you don't want to add more flour to the dough by flouring the pin, chill the pin in the freezer and the dough won't stick.

CORN

Discoloring: Some people think light-yellow corn tastes better than dark-yellow corn. To fool such people, add a dash of vinegar to the water the corn is boiling in, and the corn will turn at least a few shades lighter as it cooks. No change in taste, however.

Not enough: Yes, people expect an ear each. The answer has two parts: the culinary and the psychological. The culinary: make a filling dish that goes with the main course. A bucket of biscuits with butter and honey will do nicely. How about Lima beans with butter and brown sugar stirred in? The psychological: chop each ear of corn in half (thirds if they're quite large) and pile them in a vegetable dish. Some people will take one, some two, some three or four. But no matter what, there will always be precisely one piece left when dinner is over. (Did you think we were going to suggest succotash? We don't think you need *that* much help.)

Old, not sweet: Any corn that has been thoughtfully prehusked for you by your well-meaning supermarket probably fits into this category.

Before you cook it, slice a small piece off, and stand the ears on end in an inch of water for half an hour or so.

Whether or not you presoak, try adding ½ cup of sugar to every 2 quarts of cooking water. A tablespoon or two of corn syrup will have the same beneficial effect.

Overcooked: It is hard to imagine, in our day and age, when you can buy frozen corn on the cob that tastes almost as good as mush on a stick, that someone in your family is going to bite into a steaming ear of fresh, sweet, hot-buttered corn and say, "Good grief, Zelda-or-whatever-your-name-is, you've overcooked the corn again."

If you feel guilty, however, give in and make fresh corn soup. The amount of work required will surely absolve you:

FRESH CORN SOUP

Cooked corn
For each cup of kernels:
  1 tablespoon butter
  2 tablespoons chopped onion
  1 tablespoon flour
  1 cup milk
  Salt, pepper, nutmeg

Remove kernels from cobs. This is most of the work, unless you have a corn-grating tool. Melt butter in a heavy saucepan. Add onion and flour, and cook over medium heat for 3 minutes, stirring constantly. Warm the milk in another pot (to avoid lumps later). Stir in the corn and then the milk. Warm the mixture thoroughly, but do not boil. Season to taste with salt and pepper. Serve with a tiny sprinkling of nutmeg.

Silky: Corn silks can often be easily removed simply by holding the ear under a hard stream of water from the faucet. The corn's ear, that is, of course. Flick off the few remaining silks with a knife.

Thawed: Please see Appendix B for remarks on thawed corn that you wish was still frozen.

Too much: Except in emergencies, corn on the cob should never be reheated; it toughens the corn. Here is a simple yet interesting recipe for leftover corn on the cob:

DELAWARE CORN PUDDING

1 cup corn kernels
³/₄ cup bread crumbs
¹/₂ cup milk
1 egg yolk
¹/₂ green pepper, minced
1 egg white
2 strips bacon
Salt and pepper

Scrape off all the kernels. Mix kernels with bread crumbs, milk, egg yolk, green pepper, salt and pepper. Fold in stiffly beaten egg white. Put two strips of bacon on top and bake at 350° for 30 minutes.

CORNED BEEF

Bland: Once it's cooked, you'll just have to add a sauce with a little zip, or serve it with a particularly good mustard. Next time, add any of the following four seasonings, alone or in concert, to the cooking water for corned beef or, indeed, for boiled beef: dill seed, a 1-inch stick of cinnamon, whole celery seed, or four or five whole allspice berries.

Tough: You haven't cooked it long enough. Just keep going. It takes a long, long while to get some corned beef tender, but it eventually does happen (unless you can detect the word "Firestone" stamped into the side of the beef).

CORNSTARCH

Have none, need some: For most cooking purposes, you can substitute 2 teaspoons of regular flour for 1 teaspoon of cornstarch. In England, what we call cornstarch is actually called cornflour, and is used in some baking recipes. So there.

CRAB: *see* FISH AND SEAFOOD

CRACKERS

Not enough: Toast any kind of bread until dark (i.e., until the bread is brown, not until sunset). Using a knife with a serrated blade, saw the bread in half the hard way, making two full-sized thin sliced instead of one regular one. Cut in quarters. Instant (nearly) crackers.

Soggy: Put soggy crackers on a cookie sheet and bake for 2 or 3 minutes at 350°.

CRANBERRIES: *see* BERRIES

CREAM: *see also* MILK; SOUR CREAM; WHIPPED CREAM

Have none, need some: If you need sweet cream and have sour, baking soda sweetens sour cream. So add a pinch of soda to some sour cream and keep adding more slowly until the cream reaches the desired degree of sweetness. Start with a tiny, tiny pinch. A teaspoon per pint is the most you'd ever want to add, and rarely that much.

Or you can use powdered milk made with less water than usual, or by adding milk to the powder instead of water.

But why aren't you using your emergency can of evaporated milk? Just thought you might need a reminder—you did set those emergency supplies aside, didn't you? You can just slightly dilute the milk as a substitute for cream.

Souring: Bet you can guess if you've read the rest of this section: A pinch of baking soda will sweeten souring cream.

CREAM PUFFS

Beads of moisture: This happens when cream puffs are underbaked. Return them to the hot oven, turn off the oven at once, and let them sit in there 5 minutes, with the door slightly ajar (the traditional oven door prop is a wooden spoon). The beads of moisture should disappear.

Collapsed and soggy: Cream puffs collapse when they are cooked on the outside and too moist on the inside. So slice off the top, remove the moist dough with your fingers (yes, you can eat it), replace the top, and return to the hot oven. Turn the oven off, leave the door ajar, and wait 10 minutes. Then proceed normally.

Next time, here's the professionals' method for perfect puffs: as soon as they're cooled, put your puffs into the freezer. Even if you're serving them the same day, freeze them. When you're ready to assemble them, put them on a cookie sheet in a 350° oven for 2 minutes. Slice them in half and fill. They'll be crisp outside and soft inside, just as they should be.

Didn't puff: Make a splendid dish with crispy outsides by coating the unpuffed puffs with caramelized sugar. Toss them (using two forks) in a pot of caramelized sugar. Let them harden (which happens almost instantly) and then split them and fill as you had planned.

CREAM SOUP: *see* SOUP

CRÈME FRAÎCHE

Have none, need some: For many purposes, you can use sour cream thinned with milk or cream, especially if it is to be poured over a finished dish. If it is in a recipe that will be cooked, use gentle heat because sour cream breaks down when heated and crème fraîche doesn't.

If you have the time, you can just make your own. Here's an excerpt from a book called *Cafe Beaujolais* (by Margaret Fox and John Bear, Ten Speed Press, 1984): "It has a mellower flavor than sour cream— sort of nutty, instead of tangy. I love it, and use it in place of sour cream all the time. You can whip it and make it thicker, the same way you do with cream, or you can use it in the more liquid state."

CRÈME FRAÎCHE

Heavy cream (as many cups as you wish)
Buttermilk (1 tablespoon for each cup of heavy cream)

Combine in a saucepan over medium heat. Heat just until the chill is off—to about 50°. Pour into a glass jar, cover lightly with a piece of waxed paper, and let sit in a warm place(65° to 70°) for 12 to 20 hours, until the crème fraîche has thickened. Replace waxed paper with plastic wrap or a tight-fitting lid and refrigerate for at least 6 hours before using. Keeps up to 2 weeks.

CRISCO: *see* FAT, LARD, SHORTENING

CROQUETTES

Won't firm up: There are few things worse than a flabby croquette. Soak 1 teaspoon of gelatin in 2 tablespoons of cold water and then dissolve it over boiling water. Stir it into the croquette mix and wait until the gelatin hardens. The heat of cooking will dissolve the gelatin, and the croquette will be soft and creamy inside.

CUCUMBERS

Bland: Maybe what they need is dill seed. Try sprinkling some on sliced or marinated cucumbers or in a cucumber salad. Or maybe try celery seed.

Soggy, wilted: Put the cucumbers, whole, in a basin of cold water in the refrigerator. About an hour before you want to eat the cucumbers, peel and slice them, sprinkle them with salt, and put them back in the water. Drain before serving. As an alternative, you can make:

GWEN'S BULGARIAN CUCUMBER SOUP

1 cup plain yogurt for each ½ to 1 cup cucumbers
Salt and pepper
A few pinches of sugar
A few pinches of dill weed (fresh or dried)

Mix it all together; season to taste.

Too many: If the cucumbers are nice, firm, unshriveled, and dark green, they will keep for at least a week. If they are losing their freshness, you'd better hurry up and make something like this Norwegian dish:

BAKED STUFFED CUCUMBERS

Cucumbers
Cooked chopped meat (that includes chicken)
of any kind
Cheese of almost any kind that will melt
Bread crumbs

Boil the cucumbers for 5 minutes, unpeeled. Cut them in half the long way, scoop out the seeds, and pile on the meat. Top with the cheese and bread crumbs and bake at 350° for 30 minutes.

Another solution for excess cucumbers is to slice them fairly thick—½ inch or so—bread them, if you wish, and sauté them until brown. Turn the cucumbers over and brown the other side. You could do the same with green tomatoes and wow your friends and family with a "hot salad."

CUPCAKES: *see* CAKE

CURRY POWDER: *see also* HERBS, SPICES, SEASONINGS

Too much: If you can't or don't want to dilute the effect with more of the basic ingredient of the dish, you have two options: more rice or add things to the curry. With more rice, the curried item then becomes almost a flavoring agent. Things to serve with and add to the curry that provide a respite from the spiciness are chopped cucumber (plain or combined with plain yogurt), chopped banana, yogurt with mild vegetables chopped in it (leave the onions and garlic out this time), chopped orange or mandarin orange segments (canned is all right), or canned lychee nuts.

CUSTARDS: *see* PUDDINGS AND CUSTARDS

DATES

Stuck to each other: Put them in a warm oven for a few minutes, and they should unstick. If you're going to add them to muffins, bread, and other baked goods, cut them into the dry ingredients and toss them, so each piece is coated with flour. They're less likely to sink in clumps, as well.

Stuck to utensil: Next time dip the utensil (scissors or knife, presumably) in cold water, and cut the dates while the utensil is wet.

DISHES: *see* Appendix H: PROBLEMS WITH UTENSILS

DRINKS, ALCOHOLIC: *see* ALCOHOL

DUCK: *see* POULTRY

DUMPLINGS

Falling apart in pot: Rescue the bits from the pot (you may have to scrape some from the bottom) and transfer them to a paper-towel-lined colander. Press them, to make dry bits. Pile in a buttered dish, cover loosely with foil, and bake for 20 minutes at 350°. Serve them as baked dumplings, perhaps with a flavorful sauce.

EGGS, GENERAL: *see also* EGGS, BOILED; EGGS, DEVILED; EGGS, FRIED; EGGS, POACHED; EGGS, SCRAMBLED; EGG WHITES; EGG YOLKS; OMELETTES

Cold: Eggs should be at room temperature for baking. To bring an egg from refrigerator temperature to room temperature quickly, without cooking it in the process, dunk it in lukewarm water for 5 minutes.

Dirty: Dirty eggs are not a problem, but clean eggs often are. When you wash eggs, you remove a protective coating that was thoughtfully provided by the chicken. Cleaned eggs tend to spoil faster and to absorb refrigerator odors. If you must have clean-looking eggs, wipe them with a dry cloth. As a rule, it is best not to run raw eggs through the washing machine, unless yours has an egg cycle.

Dropped on the floor: Cover the mess with lots of salt. Then cover the salt with a bowl or pot, so the dog doesn't get into it and nobody walks through it, tracking salt and egg all over the house. In 20 minutes, the whole mess should sweep up easily with a broom and dustpan. (Does anybody have a recipe calling for egg-flavored salt?)

Eggshell in egg: Probably the simplest way to remove bits of eggshell from eggs is to use the empty half eggshell as a scoop.

Not enough: In baking, you can generally replace about one egg in three with a tablespoon of cornstarch.

Overcooked: Overcooked fried, poached, scrambled, and other such eggs tend to be tough. So why not continue cooking them until they are totally overcooked, and then use them instead of hard-boiled eggs in salads, sandwiches, and the like?

However, if your problem is that the breakfast eggs have overcooked and everyone is sitting there clamoring for breakfast, there is still hope. Make:

TRISTAN'S DAUNTLESS BAKED EGGS

For every four eggs:
   1 small can white or cheese sauce
   1/2 teaspoon Worcestershire sauce
   1 tablespoon sherry
   Croutons or shredded toast
   Any kind of cheese
   Parsley flakes

Put the eggs in a baking dish. (Peel and slice them if they are hard-boiled.) Make sauce from white or cheese sauce, Worcestershire, and sherry. Pour sauce on eggs. Sprinkle with croutons and any kind of grated cheese. Bake for 10 minutes at 325°. Sprinkle with parsley flakes just before serving. Smile.

This recipe works best with overboiled and overpoached eggs. It will still work with overfried and overscrambled, but they're not as glamorous, so you'll have to smile more.

Stuck to carton: Wet the carton and the eggs will come out without cracking.

Stuck to egg beater, pots, etc.: The secret to cleaning eggs off utensils is to use cold water, not hot water.

Too much fat in them: There's not much you can do to de-fat the egg yolk in hand, as it were, but you can often just use the whites, or mostly the egg whites, in recipes calling for whole eggs. Feed the yolks to needy pets (or just consider them the "pits" of the egg and toss them. Sure, it's extravagant, but hospitalization for a coronary is even more expensive!).

Uncertain quality: Test for freshness by lowering raw eggs into water. If they float, that means air pockets under the shell, and they are old.

Yolk in the white: When you separate eggs and there are bits of yolk in the white, it is important to remove them, because the whites may not whip unless you do. Remove the yolk with a yolk magnet, consisting of a cloth moistened in cold water. Touch it to the yolk and it will cling.

EGGS, BOILED *(see also various other* **EGG** *categories)*

Cracked before cooking: Wrap the egg very tightly in aluminum foil, twisting the ends. Then boil it normally. After boiling the egg, plunge it quickly into cold water. If you don't, it will continue to cook in the foil.

Cracked during cooking: Pour in 1 teaspoon of salt. It should keep the whites from seeping out. A few drops of lemon juice or vinegar in the egg water will have the same effect.

Crumbly, difficult to slice: If you don't have an egg-slicing gadget, the easiest way to slice hard-boiled eggs is either to use a cheese slicer or to garrote the eggs with thread. Or you can use a hot dry knife.

Difficult to peel: Tap the warm cooked egg all over the shell with a spoon, and/or roll it around in cold water. Peel it under gently running water.

Discoloring: Dark circles around the yolks of newly hard-boiled eggs can be prevented by cooking the eggs properly. Cover eggs with cool water to a height of 1 inch above the tops of the eggs. Bring rapidly to a boil. Take the pan off the heat, cover, and let stand for 20 minutes. Cool immediately in cold water.

If the eggs already have dark yolks, remove the darkness by holding the yolk under a gentle stream of cold water and lightly rubbing the yolk with your finger.

Off-center yolks: You can't change them now, but next time, roll the raw egg a couple of feet horizontally (always in the same direction) before you put it in the hot water.

Too many: Peeled hard-boiled eggs can be stored in the refrigerator for 2 or 3 days, covered by water.

Undercooked: If you have opened a soft- or medium-boiled egg in the "proper" fashion, by cutting off just a bit of the narrow end, you can cook it more by lowering it back into boiling water, suspended in cloth or cheesecloth. Don't let the water enter the egg. Alternatively, enclose your egg in a piece of foil that's big enough so you can gather the edges on top, over the opened end. Support it, vertically, in your pot between something a few minutes of boiling water won't injure (coffee mugs? cans of soup? rocks?). If this method won't work, convert your boiled egg to a scrambled or, possibly, fried egg.

EGGS, DEVILED *(see also various other* **EGG** *categories)*

Bland: Try adding crushed basil, cumin, curry, tarragon, and/or thyme to make deviled eggs a bit more devilish.

EGGS, FRIED *(see also various other* **EGG** *categories)*

Grease splattering: Sprinkle cornstarch on the pan or griddle. This is said to impart a nice flavor to the eggs, as well.

Overcooked: *see* **EGGS, GENERAL, Overcooked**

EGGS, POACHED *(see also various other* **EGG** *categories)*

Overcooked: *see* **EGGS, GENERAL, Overcooked**

Runny: A few drops of vinegar in the water will help keep poached eggs from running all over the pot.

A famous egg chef (thank you, Mary Ann G.) taught us that if you make a little whirlpool or vortex in the water, using a spoon or a stick, and drop the raw egg insides right into the center of the vortex, it will all stay together instead of running around the pot.

EGGS, SCRAMBLED *(see also various other* **EGG** *categories)*

Bland: In addition to all the "usual" stuff, like onions and mushrooms and tomatoes and spinach, consider the following seasonings, all of which are compatible with scrambled eggs: crushed basil, chervil, ground cloves, cumin, curry, marjoram, toasted poppy seed, rosemary, tarragon, thyme, and turmeric.

Overcooked: (1) Chop up to use on salads, for garnishes, or in egg salad. *See also* **EGGS, GENERAL, Overcooked**. (2) Put on toast, sprinkle with cheese, and run under the broiler until the cheese melts.

Tough: Salt helps make cooked eggs tough. Next time, add the salt after cooking. (Pepper doesn't have this effect.)

EGG WHITES: *see also* **EGGS, GENERAL**

Not enough: Before beating, add 1 teaspoon of cream of tartar for each cup of egg whites. They will beat up fluffier, thus having greater volume.

Too many: Freeze them, one to an ice cube tray section. When they are frozen, remove them from the tray and store them in a plastic bag in the freezer. They will last for months.

Won't whip: The eggs should be at least 3 days removed from the chicken. If you got them at a supermarket, they probably are. They should also be at room temperature. Either let them sit for ½ hour or dunk them in lukewarm water for 5 minutes.

The beaters must be very clean and free of grease; even a tiny bit may retard whipping.

And if you've done all that and they still won't whip, add a pinch of baking soda or, less desirably, a pinch of salt. The whites may be a bit fluffier than usual, but they will whip.

EGG YOLKS

Left over: If unbroken, cover with water or milk. They will last for 2 or 3 days in the refrigerator. If broken or unbroken but more than 2 or 3 days old, freeze them. Stabilize them with a tiny pinch of salt or sugar (depending on your probable future use of them) for each yolk. Consider freezing them separately, perhaps in an ice cube tray, for future use one at a time.

Those of us lowering our fat intake tend to accumulate egg yolks. They are still good food and unparalleled for making a crust rich-looking and shiny (without adding too much fat). If you've many accumulated yolks, do you have a dog or cat? An egg yolk every few days is good for the coat. Or you can beat an egg yolk into a few tablespoons of your shampoo (just before using, please). Some people swear it "feeds" the hair without going through the digestive tract. Hmm.

EGGPLANT

Bitter: The peel is the bitter part. So, one way or another, try to remove it. One way: See **Difficult to peel**, this section. Another: Using a 12-gauge shotgun . . . oh, never mind.

Bland: There are those who feel that the best way to improve an eggplant is to encase it in cement and drop it in the river. For those who disagree with this sentiment, here are some seasonings that will improve the flavor of a bland eggplant: basil, celery seed, chervil, oregano, sage, and thyme. If you're breading, put the spices in the breading. If you're frying, sprinkle on before cooking.

Difficult to peel: If you wish to remove the skin from your eggplant to fry it or something, try slicing it first and then cutting the skin off the slices with a pair of scissors. If you want to end up with mashed eggplant, consider charring the skin. Hold the eggplant over an open flame (the gas range works fine for this), skewered on a big fork, until the skin is blackened all over. This takes a while, so arm yourself with a good paperback book to read. When it looks done, put it in a small paper bag and let it sit for 15 minutes. Then rub the skin off under running water. If it needs further cooking, you can steam it or bake it or slice and sauté it. The smoky flavor is in the flesh and won't wash away.

Discoloring: If a sliced eggplant should start to discolor, drop it in salt-water to retard the discoloration.

FAT, LARD, SHORTENING

Difficult to get out of can: When Crisco or other such fats get down toward the bottom of the can, fill the can with boiling water, cool it, and the shortening will float to the top, enabling you to utilize it down (up?) to the last drop.

Smelly: To remove odors from frying fat that you'd like to reuse, fry potato slices in it until they are brown. The potato will sop up all the extraneous odors, even powerful ones like fish and onion. Why not do the potatoes last, and have a fish-and-chips dinner?

Splattering: A dash of salt or cornstarch will often stop fat from splattering.

FIGS

Bland: Try powdered cinnamon or rosemary water (¼ teaspoon in ¼ cup of boiling water; remove from heat, let cook; strain out the rosemary, and pour the water onto the figs). Or stir ¼ teaspoon of powdered cardamom into ½ cup of honey and spoon over the figs.

Stuck together: When dried figs stick together, heat the whole she-bang in the oven at 300° for a few minutes; they will come unstuck.

FISH AND SEAFOOD

Bland: Just about any herb or spice you
have in the house can be used in some
fashion on most fish dishes. Just to help
you get started thinking about this, here is a
partial list of relevant seasonings, with occasional comments:

allspice (four or five whole berries in the cooking water)

anise (good with cod)

basil (for broiled or scalloped fish)

bay leaf

chervil

cinnamon (try it in bouillon, but go light at first)

coriander (baked or broiled fish)

curry

dill weed

fennel

garlic

ginger (on broiled fish, use dried or grated fresh ginger)

mace (with trout)

marjoram (broiled, baked, or creamed fish)

mustard (fried or baked fish)

nutmeg

oregano

paprika

rosemary (salmon)

saffron (sauces)

savory

sesame seed (fried, broiled, baked fish)

tarragon (lobster, tuna, salmon)

Go wild.

Breading falls off: *see* **BREADING, Falls off**

Dry: Serve with a sauce, or, simply, melted butter and slivered almonds.

Canny flavor: To make canned fish (crab, tuna, salmon, etc.) taste uncanny, soak it in fresh whatever-liquid-it-was-packed-in (either oil or water, presumably) for about half an hour.

Gamey flavor: Some fish taste too gamey for some people. A sauce involving brandy, sherry, or ginger lessens the gaminess.

Overcooked: "When you overcook a fish," someone's grandmother must have said, "boil the hell out of it and make fish stock." Check your cookbooks for all the wondrous things to do with fish stock, among which, for instance, is:

SAUCE VELOUTÉ

1 cup fish stock
2 tablespoons butter
2 tablespoons flour
Capers, mashed anchovies, or mashed sardines (optional)

Mix the ingredients together. You can pour the sauce directly onto any fish, right there on the plate, or you can create a casserole by pouring the sauce over some bland cooked fish. Add boiled, sliced potatoes if you wish, and heat at 350° for 20 minutes.

If you have the time, overcooked fish can be made into fish cakes or croquettes. The binding sauce will restore some moisture.

Salty: When raw fish (or shrimp) is too salty, soak it in clear water for about 10 minutes. If you aren't going to serve it soon, store it in new water, not the water you just soaked it in.

Adding a lot of vinegar (1 cup per quart of liquid) to the cooking water helps cut down on saltiness while cooking fish.

Scaly: If an allegedly scaled fish still has scales on it, and you don't feel like hiking back to the fish seller to trade it in, try plunging the fish into scalding water, then into cold water, and then scraping off the now-loosened scales with a serrated knife (such as a grapefruit knife).

Shellfish, difficult to shell: Next time, cook shrimp, crayfish, or other shellfish in water to which you have added 1 tablespoon white wine vinegar for each quart of water. The flesh will be firmer without over-cooking, and you will find the shells easier to remove. This time, try peeling them under running warm water, letting the water help detach the shells.

Smelly: In frying fish, the more dreadful smells usually come from the hot fat, not from the fish itself. Reduce the heat and see if that doesn't help.

When poaching fish, add some celery leaves to the pot. They will help destroy the fish smell (not entirely, however; who wants a fish that smells like celery?), and smell pretty good themselves.

In general, a caramel type of odor tends to neutralize fishy odors. So either issue caramels to your guests, or burn some granulated sugar in a pan. Either use a disposable pan, or line a regular saucepan with aluminum foil to avoid a messy clean-up job.

Strong: Boiled fish sometimes tastes too fishy. Let it stand in the cooking water or sauce after it is cooked, and the flavor will dissipate somewhat.

Too much: If it is already cooked, make timbales, croquettes, fish cakes, or even (for firm-fleshed fish) a salad.

FLAMBÉED DISHES: *see* ALCOHOL, Brandy or liqueur won't ignite

FLOUR (ALL-PURPOSE)

Have none, need some: For 1 cup of all-purpose flour, you can substitute 1 cup plus 2 tablespoons of cake flour. In many baking situations, 1½ cups of rolled oats can replace 1 cup of all-purpose flour. Consider whirling your oatmeal in the food processor to change its texture if you're trying this.

FOWL: *see* POULTRY

FRANKFURTERS: *see* SAUSAGES

FRENCH TOAST: *see* PANCAKES

FROSTING: *see* ICING

FROZEN FOODS: *see specific foods; also* APPENDIX B

FRUIT: *see specific fruit*

FRUITCAKE: *see also* CAKE

Old and dry: Cut deep slits in the top and pour in brandy or sherry to taste. Wrap the cake in plastic and let it stand overnight to let it all sink in.

FUDGE: *see* CANDY

GARLIC

Difficult to peel: Here are four things to try: (1) If the peel is slightly loose, run hot water over the garlic, and the peel should come off readily. (2) Cut off the root end of the garlic cloves (the flattish end at the bottom of the bulb). Mash them with the side of a big kitchen knife. The peels and insides should be easy to separate. (3) If you need whole cloves and you've got a little time, drop the garlic into boiling water for 5 seconds; then drop it in cold water. Now the peel should come off easily. (4) Margaret Fox (in our joint venture book, *Cafe Beaujolais*) reports that one can slice off the stem of a garlic bulb, separate it into cloves, heat just enough olive oil to cover the cloves to 230°, turn off the heat, and add the garlic. After 15 seconds, test one clove; it should easily pop out of its skin. Drain the oil. Peel all the garlic. To save, return the peeled garlic to cooled oil and store in a covered container. Eventually, use the oil to make a great salad dressing.

GELATIN

Stuck in mold: Loosen the gelatin around the edges with the tip of a knife. Dip the mold in hot water (not so far that the water runs onto the gelatin) for a few seconds, invert it on a plate, and shake the mold off slowly. If it is still stuck, repeat. If it is *still* stuck, give up. Perhaps you used library paste instead of gelatin powder. (Next time, lightly oil the mold before adding the gelatin.)

Time is short: If you don't even have time to follow the "quick method" given on most boxes, try this "even quicker" method, which may be up to 50 percent faster. Add just enough hot water to the powder to dissolve it. A few tablespoons should be enough. Then use ice water for the rest of the liquid. If you add fruits, they should be very cold.

Too thick: If a gelatin dessert sets too long and you wanted to have stirred in fruits or marbles or something and now you can't, warm it up by any convenient means (oven, stove, setting it in a bowl of warm water), and it will thinnen (which is the opposite of thicken). Then let it set again to the right consistency for stirring stuff in.

Too thin: If a gelatin dessert or salad won't thicken at all, or not fast enough for you, set it in an ice bath. An ice bath is a big bowl full of ice cubes. Next time, be sure you have let the gelatin soak in cold liquid for 5 minutes before using it.

GOOSEBERRIES: *see* BERRIES

GOULASH: *see* STEW

GRAPEFRUIT

Difficult to get the white stuff off: When you've peeled a grapefruit and there is still a lot of white stuff on it, you can either scrape at the white stuff with the edge of your serrated grapefruit knife, or you can dunk the grapefruit in hot water for 2 minutes. Next time, boil the grapefruit for 5 minutes before peeling and all the white stuff will come away with the peel.

Difficult to peel: Pour boiling water over the grapefruit and let it stand for 5 minutes in the water. It should then peel readily. You can dunk it in cold water if it's too hot to handle. The peel won't reattach, we promise.

Sour: Curiously enough, a bit of salt has the effect of making sour grapefruit taste sweeter.

Unjuicy: If there are two of you (people, not grapefruits), stand at opposite ends of the room and roll the grapefruits back and forth for a few minutes. Rolling it around on a tabletop in a circular motion (like making balls out of clay) will have the same effect, although it is not nearly as much fun. Another option is to cook the grapefruit in a microwave oven, at medium heat, for 15 seconds.

GRAVY

Bland, flat, pallid, grey: Depending on the kind of gravy, consider adding any of the following five kinds of ingredients:

1. Herbs and spices; for instance, ground allspice, coriander, marjoram, mustard, savory, or thyme.

2. Extracts, such as bouillon cubes, yeast extracts, or meat extracts.

3. Alcohol, of which sherry and port are most traditional, but white vermouth is an interesting variation.

4. Bottled mixed seasonings, such as soy sauce, Tabasco, Worcestershire, A-1, and so on.

5. Red currant jelly can be added to meat gravy.

Fatty: If the fat is mostly on the top, you can either skim it off or sop it up with a piece of bread. If you're being fanatical, let it stand. While it's sending the fat up to the top, tear paper toweling into wide strips. Float these on top, one at a time, drawing them off toward the edge. They'll remove the last traces of fat. If the fat is in the middle (and isn't that the case with most of us?), the easiest thing to do is to chill the gravy (quickly in the freezer, if necessary), skim the fat off, and reheat it. Next time, you may wish to get one of those clever gravy boats, in which the spout goes to the bottom, so you are pouring from the lean bottom of the gravy rather than the fatty top.

Lumpy: Beat lumpy gravy with a whisk or with a rotary (hand-operated) beater. Use a blender or food processor only as a last resort. Or pour (or force) the gravy through a wire strainer. Delumping gravy may make it too thin, in which case see **GRAVY, Too thin.**

Not brown enough: To darken gravy quickly without affecting the flavor, add 1 teaspoon of instant coffee.

Not enough: If there aren't enough drippings left in the pan to make any gravy at all, add 1 cup of water and a bouillon cube to whatever is in the pan, and cook until the cube is dissolved.

If you have some gravy but not enough, either add one of the many kinds of canned gravies available, or try this very fast substitute: For ½ cup of gravy, add 1 teaspoon of meat-flavoring sauce (e.g., Worcestershire or A-1) and 1 teaspoon of lemon juice to one 8-ounce can of tomato sauce.

Salty: The only certain way to decrease saltiness is to increase quantity. A few pinches of brown sugar often have the effect of overcoming saltiness without sweetening. Or, for minor oversalting, cut up a raw potato into thin slices and cook them in the gravy until they become translucent.

Too thin: The best thickening agent is time. (Not thyme, time.) As a gravy cooks, the water evaporates, but not the other ingredients, so it becomes thicker. If you don't have time, or you can't afford to reduce the quantity, here are the most common thickening agents:

Arrowroot (about 1 tablespoon per cup of liquid, dissolved in cold water, then stirred in within 10 minutes of serving; can be done just before serving, since arrowroot has no taste of its own).

Cornstarch (about 1 to 1½ teaspoons per cup of liquid dissolved in cold water, then added. Allow time for gravy to cook and overcome the cornstarchy taste).

Other thickeners for various situations are rice, barley, a paste of flour and water (also good for scrapbooks and papier-mâché), milk, cream, egg yolks (remember the ones you put in the freezer?), mashed potato flakes, and (ugh) blood (preferably that of a bird or animal, not the chef, added just before serving). Here comes the most helpful suggestion on this page: never boil blood!

GREEN BEANS: *see* BEANS, LIMA AND STRING

GREEN ONIONS: *see* ONIONS

GREEN PEPPERS

Bland: Sprinkle with celery seed or a tiny bit (⅛ teaspoon per pepper) of fennel.

Need to destem: Instead of cutting around the stem, turn the pepper stem side down, cut most of the way through, break it the rest of the way, and easily break the stem away from whichever half it stayed with.

GREENS

Bland: For cooked greens, try adding one or more of these: mace, marjoram, or rosemary to the cooking water; or a sprinkling of poppy seed or sesame seed on the finished product. Do you like vinegar? Balsamic vinegar sprinkled on hot greens is tasty!

For raw greens, add anise (about ¼ teaspoon, crushed, per 4 servings), basil, chervil, caraway, or savory.

Difficult to separate: If you can't separate the leaves of a lettuce or other tightly packed green vegetable easily, hit the stem end sharply on the counter; then twist out the core (it should come out easily if you hit it hard enough), and run cold water vigorously into the hole you have created. The leaves will separate beautifully, not unlike a leafy green peacock.

Dirty: Wash in warm water to loosen the dirt, eggs, nits, bugs, and worms. Now that you've learned what might have been in your greens, you've probably thrown them in the garbage and bought some nice canned lettuce. Not to worry. Washing really works. (If they are especially dirty, you can even add some mild soap to the water.) Rinse well in cold water (at least four times if you've used soap) until clean.

Rusting: If your lettuce or other greens are looking rusty, store them in a plastic bag along with a couple of paper napkins to absorb the excess moisture, which is the problem. Some supermarkets drench their greens. They look dewy, but they rot in a few days when you bring them home. Drain such greens well before refrigerating with those paper towels.

Smelly: If cooking greens get too smelly for your taste (or nose), add some salt to the cooking water and cook uncovered.

Spinach is too spinachy: Nothing else is quite as spinachy as spinach. If your spinach is too spinachy, de-spinach it by adding some curry powder: about ½ teaspoon to a package of frozen spinach. If it still tastes bad, try just a little crushed pineapple. Honest.

Wet: For regular loosely packed greens, let them drip into a colander; wrap them lightly in an absorbent towel, and chill. For Bibb and other full-headed greens, place them on a Turkish towel, cover with a plain towel, and chill for an hour or two.

If you need greens right away, and they're wet, throw them in a pillowcase and spin them dry on the spin cycle of your washing machine for a minute or two.

Wilted: If you've got an hour, dip the greens in hot water, then in ice water with a dash of vinegar. Shake the excess liquid from them, and chill the lettuce in the refrigerator for 1 hour.

If you need them right away, unwilt them by tossing them with a few drops of oil to coat the leaves before adding dressing.

For hopelessly wilted greens, try this interesting recipe for hopelessly wilted greens:

MEREDITH'S HOPELESSLY WILTED GREENS DISH

Slices bacon
¼ cup French dressing
¼ teaspoon celery salt
2 tablespoons chopped chives
2 tablespoons vinegar
1 tablespoon sugar

Tear the wilted greens into bite-size pieces and put them on a plate. Sauté the bacon and chop it into small bits. Mix the bacon with the French dressing, celery salt, chives, vinegar, and sugar, and bring to a boil in the bacon skillet. Pour this sauce over the greens. Put the plate of greens with sauce on top of a bowl of hot water, and warm gently for 6 minutes. Toss and serve.

H

HAM

Curling: If slices of ham are starting to curl under the broiler, make a slice through the fat on the edge every inch or so. You can do this quickly and easily with scissors. It is the fat that curls, not the meat.

Salty: Slice the ham. Soak the slices in milk for 15 to 30 minutes, then wash them off in cold water. This won't affect the taste of the ham at all, except to make it less salty.

HAMBURGERS

Bland: Mix any of the following seasonings in with the ground meat at a rate of roughly 1 to 2 teaspoons per pound: ground allspice, celery seed, cumin, garlic powder, nutmeg, oregano, or sesame seed.

If the hamburgers are already cooked and you want to do something more inspiring than drowning them in store-bought hamburger sauce (ketchup), here are a few inspirations:

Cover them with guacamole, pizza sauce, bacon crumbles, shredded Cheddar cheese mixed with chopped walnuts, raisin sauce, curry sauce plus chutney, sautéed onions, sour cream plus horseradish, a mound of diced stuffed green olives, or chili plus sliced black olives.

Or try one of these truly inspirational hamburgers:

HAMBURGERS BLEU

Put a dollop of thick blue or Roquefort cheese dressing on the top of your cooked hamburgers. Add some crumbles of blue cheese and a strip of something red—like pimento or tomato. Broil for 3 minutes.

HAMBURGERS ROUGE

1 small can pineapple bits
1 heaping tablespoon ketchup
1 tablespoon vinegar
1 teaspoon soy sauce
¼ cup cold water

Mix together pineapple, ketchup, vinegar, and soy sauce. Thicken with cornstarch dissolved in ¼ cup cold water. Heat until thick and gooey. Pour over cooked hamburgers, and toss a few nuts on top.

Stuck to fingers: Dip your fingers in cold water first and raw meat won't stick to them while you're molding meatballs or sculpting replicas of the Venus de Milo, or whatever it is *you* do with ground round.

HANDS: *see* Appendix H, Hands (your very own)

HERBS, SPICES, SEASONINGS

Clogged: Salt shakers clog when the salt becomes moist. Overcome this problem by putting ½ teaspoon of raw rice or a tiny bit of blotter paper into the salt shaker. Or mix about 1 tablespoon of cornstarch into a normal-sized box of salt; it will pour freely.

Put about ½ teaspoon of whole peppers into a pepper shaker, and it will not only keep the pepper pouring, it will also impart a lovely fresh-pepper smell, if your nose can detect that sort of thing.

Have one kind, need another: For most herbs and spices, 1 teaspoon of fresh equals ⅓ to ½ teaspoon of dried.

Old, weak: Many herbs lose their potency after a few months; most in a year. One way to deal with old herbs is to rub them between your fingers for a few moments. Some spices can be renewed, if it ties in with your recipe, by cooking them in butter for a few minutes before using. This method is especially effective with curry powder, for instance.

HOLLANDAISE SAUCE: *see* SAUCES

HONEY

Crystallized, sugared: Heating honey will restore it to its uncrystallized state, just the way it came out of the bee. A simple way to heat it is to stand your honeypot in a pan of hot water. A faster way is to cook the honey in a microwave oven for 60 to 90 seconds per cup of honey, on a high setting.

Have none, need some: In most recipes, you can substitute 1¼ cups of sugar and ¼ cup of any liquid for 1 cup of honey.

Stuck to container: Next time, butter the container lightly before pouring the honey in; it won't stick at all.

HOT DOGS: *see* SAUSAGES

I

ICE CREAM

Icy: When ice cream stored in the freezer starts to get icy or crystallized, you can often cure the problem by wrapping it very tightly in aluminum foil and returning it to the freezer at least overnight.

Melted: It is probably safer not to refreeze melted ice cream, and if you do, it tastes pretty dreadful anyway. What, then, do you do with it? Here are a few suggestions:

Use it on fruit as a cream sauce, if the flavors seem compatible.

Pour it on chunks of toasted pound cake, for a Backward Sundae (the ice cream is the topping).

Or save it in the refrigerator until tomorrow morning and serve it with hot or cold cereal for a breakfast the kids will never forget.

ICE CUBES

Air bubbles: Are you sure you don't have enough to worry about? All right, next time boil the water first, pour it in the tray, let it cool to room temperature, and then put it in the freezer. No bubbles.

ICING

Gooey: Gooey icing is difficult to spread unless you dip the knife in very hot water before spreading and again during the spreading process, as necessary.

Lumpy: Icing can be lumpy because of lumps in the sugar or defects in your spreading technique. Do the best you can. A smooth (not serrated) knife dipped in hot water may make the process easier. Or you can cover the lumpy icing with chopped nuts, or chopped or shaved chocolate, or drizzle a thin chocolate glaze over the frosted cake in a criss-cross pattern, letting it run down the sides. This confuses the eye and pleases the tongue.

Sugary: When boiled icing starts becoming sugary as it cooks, add a few drops of vinegar. This will retard the sugaring process but won't change the taste at all.

Too thick: If the icing is already made and too thick, stir in some cream until the consistency is right.

If it gets too thick while being made, beat or stir in a few drops of lemon juice or boiling water until it becomes thinner.

Too thin: Add sugar (preferably confectioners' sugar) a very little at a time, stirring madly or beating as you do.

If, for some reason, you don't want to add sugar, beat the icing wherever there is indirect heat: in the hot sun, near an open oven door, or in the top of a double boiler.

JELL-O: *see* **GELATIN**

KALE: *see* **GREENS**

KETCHUP: *see* **SAUCES**

LAMB

Bland: Lamb is probably as compatible with as wide a variety of seasonings as anything in the supermarket. Consider, among others, the following: ground allspice, caraway seeds (especially in stew), chervil, cloves (add five or six to the marinade), coriander (sparingly— ¼ teaspoon per 4 servings), cumin, dill seed, ginger, juniper berries (crush them and rub them into the lamb), mace, oregano, rosemary, or tarragon.

Lamb chops curling: Slash the fat on the edges every half inch or so, and turn the chops over at once (you can turn them back later).

Mutton fat tastes "sheepy": Mutton fat is great to cook with when it doesn't taste too strong. If it is too strong, add 1 part lard to 2 parts fat, chop it all up together, and melt it in a double boiler with ¼ of its bulk in skim milk, and toss in some sweet herbs (e.g., basil, marjoram, anise, and/or mint).

Muttony: When lamb tastes too strong or too muttony, try the following de-muttonizing marinade. Wipe lamb with a damp cloth and rub with the juice of one lemon plus 2 tablespoons of olive oil. Let stand for 2 hours before cooking. Use garlic when you cook it.

LARD: *see* FAT, LARD, SHORTENING

LEMON

Dried up, old, unjuicy: Boil the lemon for about 5 minutes and a lot more juice will come out: roughly ⅓ more. (It is better, but not vital, to let the lemon cool in the refrigerator before juicing.) Heating for 5 minutes in a 300° oven will have the same effect, and so will 15 seconds on a high setting in a microwave oven. So, to a lesser extent, will rolling the lemon around on a tabletop with a circular pressing motion, as in making balls of clay.

Have none, need some: For small quantity use, ½ teaspoon of vinegar can be substituted for 1 teaspoon of lemon juice.

Pits falling in: Wrap half a lemon in cheesecloth before squeezing. For serving at dinner, do as some elegant restaurants do: knot or sew the cheesecloth shut. Very classy.

Squirting: The current world's record is held by a lady from Nashville, Tennessee, who shot a stream of lemon juice 48 feet 2 inches, or across the entire width of the dance floor of the Gilded Gazebo Supper Club. Good etiquette requires you to prevent squirting by inserting a fork into your lemon wedge and squeezing it over the fork, shielding it with your hand as you do so.

LETTUCE: *see* GREENS

LIMA BEANS: *see* BEANS, LIMA AND STRING

LIQUEUR: *see* ALCOHOL

LIVER

Bland: Liver, especially beef liver, isn't too compatible with herbs and spices, although caraway seeds and juniper berries (crushed and rubbed in) do have a pleasant effect. It is better to serve the bland liver with an appropriate yummy sauce. Two sauces for beef liver and one for chicken livers are given herewith:

CREOLE SAUCE FOR BEEF LIVER

- **8 ounces tomato sauce**
- **2 tablespoons vinegar**
- **1 tablespoon brown sugar**
- **¼ cup chopped onion**
- **¼ cup chopped green pepper**
- **1 minced clove garlic**

Mix it all up together, heat through, and pour it on the liver.

MR. P.'S BEEF-LIVER SAUCE

¹/₄ cup boiling water
³/₄ cup peanut butter (smooth or chunky)
2 teaspoons garlic salt
¹/₈ teaspoon cayenne pepper
Toasted sesame seeds (optional)

Stir the boiling water into the peanut butter to loosen it.
Add garlic salt and cayenne, and, optionally, top with
toasted sesame seeds.

SOUR-CREAM SAUCE FOR CHICKEN LIVERS

For each pound of chicken livers:
1 cup sour cream
2 teaspoons lemon juice plus 1 teaspoon chervil
or
Dried dill weed
or
1 tablespoon tomato purée plus 1 teaspoon oregano

Mix all the ingredients and warm them up slowly in a heavy
pan over low heat. Pour the sauce over your livers.

Popping, splattering: Chicken livers are wont to do this, but they
won't if you perforate them all over with a fork.

Tough: No matter what the instructions may say, meat tenderizer works
as well on liver as on most other kinds of meats.

If you anticipate that your liver is going to be tough or untasty, soak
it for an hour in either milk or red wine, according to your taste, and
fry it in butter.

LOBSTER: *see* FISH AND SEAFOOD

LOGANBERRIES: *see* BERRIES

MACARONI: *see* PASTA

MANGOES

Difficult to peel: All mangoes are difficult to peel from one end and easy to peel from the other end. As the famous calypso song goes, "If your mango hard to peel/I got for you, mon, such a deal/If this side doesn't work my friend/Simply try the other end." If you have a really reluctant mango, try a vegetable peeler. Last resort: use a serrated knife, sawing back and forth very carefully. Hold the mango in a dish towel (so it doesn't slip) over a sink (in case it drips).

Unripe: Put unripe mangoes in a paper bag and keep them in a dark, warm place until they ripen. Ripe mangoes are normally a bright yellow-orange.

MARSHMALLOWS

Hard, stale: Seal them up in an airtight place (like a plastic bag) with a slice of fresh bread for 3 days, and you will have fresh marshmallows and stale bread.

Stuck to utensil while cutting: Dip the scissors (you were using scissors, weren't you?) in cold water and cut while the blades are still wet.

MAYONNAISE

Curdled: Place one egg yolk in a clean, cold, dry bowl. Add the mayonnaise very, very slowly (no, even slower than that), stirring as you add. Alternatively, add boiling water to the curdled mayonnaise, 1 tablespoon at a time, stirring as you add. (Note: mayonnaise is much more likely to curdle on a humid day.)

Not enough: In things like egg salad or on sandwiches, stir in some ketchup or chile sauce, if the taste is compatible. If not, thin out the mayonnaise (see **MAYONNAISE, Too thick**) and increase the seasoning in the salad. Or make your own mayonnaise; it's unbelievably easy in a blender or food processor. Here's how:

MAYONNAISE

1 egg
½ teaspoon powdered mustard
¼ teaspoon salt
2 tablespoons vinegar
1 cup salad oil

Combine egg, mustard, salt, vinegar, and ¼ cup of the salad oil in a blender or food processor. Turn on the blender (low) or food processor. Uncover or open pouring lid and pour in remaining oil in a fine steady stream. Now you have mayonnaise—about 1¼ cups.

Separated: Rinse a bowl in hot water and dry it. Add 1 teaspoon of prepared mustard, 1 teaspoon of mayonnaise, and beat with a whisk until creamy. Add another teaspoon of mayonnaise, and repeat. And so on, 1 teaspoon at a time.

Too thick: Thin it out with cream, whipped cream, evaporated milk, or lemon juice, whichever is handy. None of these will flavor the mayonnaise. If you would like to flavor it, you can thin it out with fruit juice. The juice from a cantaloupe or watermelon is especially interesting. To lower the fat content, consider using nonfat sour cream or yogurt in a mayonnaise dressing for part of the mayonnaise.

MEAT: *see specific kinds, for example,* LAMB, PORK, POULTRY

MEAT LOAF

Bland: All of these seasonings (used one or two at a time, please) go nicely with meat loaf: ground allspice, celery seed, coriander, fennel, garlic powder, nutmeg, oregano, paprika, and sesame seed. Also see the next suggestion.

Stuck to the pan: This time, scrape it out as best you can with a spatula and reassemble it, using sauce to hold it together.

Next time, put a strip or two of partly cooked bacon underneath the meat loaf before cooking and it will not only not stick, but it also won't taste bacon-flavored. If you want it to taste bacon-flavored, drape the rest of that bacon package over the top. This qualifies as de-blanding, too.

MERINGUE

Difficult to cut: Dip the knife in very cold water.

Disintegrating, cracked: Best to make a pavlova, the New Zealand national dessert. Assemble the bits in a ring, using a liberal amount of whipped cream to stick it together. Fill the ring with whipped cream. Top with fresh fruit (kiwi, berries, or well-drained mandarin orange slices).

Weeping: We hate to see a grown meringue cry. It tends to do so when it is cooled too fast. Cool it very slowly, by leaving it in the oven as the oven cools for instance, and it will weep no more.

MILK: *see also* CREAM

Have none, need some: If you don't have powdered milk on your emergency shelf, then for most uses (including drinking, but especially cooking) you can substitute the following for 1 cup of whole milk: 1 cup buttermilk plus ½ teaspoon of baking soda, or 1 cup of skim milk plus 2 teaspoons of oil or fat. If you need sour milk, add 1 teaspoon of lemon juice or cider vinegar to 1 cup of regular milk.

In baking, depending on the recipe, 1 cup of fruit juice can sometimes be substituted for 1 cup of milk. Apple juice is the most neutral-tasting.

Souring: Add 2 teaspoons of baking soda to a quart of milk and it will be good for another day or two. This is the lactic equivalent of putting a penny in the fuse.

MOLASSES

Stuck to container: Next time butter the container lightly before putting the molasses in it, and the molasses will roll right off. Now, put the container in a larger container with hot water in it. Warmed molasses is thinner and will unstick.

MOUSSE

Doesn't set: It isn't a mousse any more; it is now a sauce to serve over an appropriate fruit or cubed bland cake. It's a great sauce, probably.

MUFFINS: *see also* BREAD AND ROLLS

Soggy bottoms: This happens because the moisture in the muffins condenses in the bottom of the muffin pan after cooking. Counteract either by putting the muffins on a rack to cool or by simply turning them sideways in their little compartments when you take them out of the oven to cool.

Stuck to the muffin pan: Put the muffin pan on a wet towel. In a couple of minutes, the muffins should come free.

Tough: Tough muffins (which are not the same as tough cookies) get that way because you probably beat the dough rather than folded it over and over. This time, cut your tough muffins in slices, toast, and serve with jam. Next time, fold the dough.

MUSHROOMS

Bland: The best seasoning to bring out the flavor in mushrooms is marjoram. Add a generous dash to cooking mushrooms. No marjoram? Excuse me, have you got the thyme?

Darkening; too dark: Wipe them with a damp cloth, rub them with lemon juice, and store them in the refrigerator. Or steam them in milk or butter in the top of a double boiler for 20 minutes. Or, while cooking, add a few drops of lemon juice to the cooking liquid. (It is just about impossible to lighten mushrooms in a black iron skillet.)

Shriveled: Peel them with your fingers. Beneath every shriveled mushroom there lies a somewhat smaller smooth mushroom waiting to be found. (Use the peelings to flavor soup or sauces.)

Too light: Mushrooms will darken if cooked in butter in a black iron skillet on high heat.

Too many: Chop them, cook very slowly over low heat until they are reduced by half or more. Now you have duxelle, a mushroom paste that stores well (in the refrigerator). Use it where mushroom flavoring is required, for example, in sauces, soups, and stews.

MUSHROOM SOUP: *see* SOUPS

MUSSELS: *see also* CLAMS; OYSTERS

Uncertain quality: Steam mussels for 10 minutes. If they open up, they're good. If they don't, they're bad.

MUSTARD GREENS: *see* GREENS

NECTARINES

Unripe: To accelerate ripening, store them in an airtight paper bag for 1 or 2 days. Set them where the sun can warm the bag.

NOODLES: *see* PASTA

NUTS

Crumbly: If nut meats crumble when you crack the shells, soak the remaining unshelled nuts in salt water overnight.

Difficult to crack, shell: For pecans and similar nuts, cover them with boiling water and let stand until cold. Crack the nuts end-to-end with a nutcracker and the meat should emerge in one piece.

For chestnuts and similar nuts, make a small gash on the flat side the nut, penetrating the outer skin. Roast in a 400° oven until the skins loosen, or cover with cold water and bring to a boil. Remove and let stand until cool enough to handle. The shells and skins should be much easier to handle.

Difficult to peel, skin, remove nut meat: For almonds and similar nuts, drop the whole nut (shelled) in boiling water, and let stand for 3 minutes with the heat off. The skins (that is, the brown layer on the nut meat) should come off easily. Dry the nut meats on a towel.

Have none, need some: In brownies and other such, coarse bran can successfully be substituted for nuts.

In molasses cake, spice cake, and other stuff of that ilk, brown a cup of rolled oats by spreading on a cookie sheet in a 425° oven (watch carefully), and add before baking.

Shells mixed in with nuts: Dump the whole works in a bowl of water. The shells will float, the meat will sink, and the guppies will swim around in the middle.

OATS

Have none, need some: In baking, 1 cup of all-purpose flour can replace 1⅓ cups of oats. If you have any cereal flakes, consider substituting those. Cornflake-raisin cookies are not bad at all, as long as you don't apologize while serving them.

OATMEAL: *see* CEREAL

OLIVES

Hard to pit: Place them on a paper towel or wax paper. Roll gently with a rolling pin. Press the olive with the heel of your hand and the pit will pop out.

OMELETTES: *see also* EGGS *(various subcategories)*

Stuck to pan: Remove the eggs as best you can, probably with a wooden implement (no, not your cane), and either (a) cover the bits with an appropriate sauce or (b) save them as a garnish on dishes such as fried rice.

Next time, grease the pan with unsalted butter. Salted butter is more likely to cause things to stick.

ONIONS

Bland: Powdered basil, ginger, sage, and thyme are all good things to add to bland cooking onions—or just butter and lightly sugar them.

Crying while peeling or slicing: The best antidote for most people is coldness. If you have time, chill the onions in the freezer for 10 to 15 minutes or more before slicing. Alternatively, you can peel them under water (just the onion and your hands; no scuba gear needed) or under cold running water. Finally, for some people, biting on a piece of bread seems to help, for others not at all. Those of us desperately sensitive to chopping onions have been known to use our snorkeling goggles when chopping many onions, or even use the food processor for just one onion (the clean-up is worth it).

Difficult to peel: Hot water loosens onion peels. Drop onions in boiling water for somewhere between 10 seconds (for tiny white onions) to 5 minutes (for big old red ones) and then dip them in cold water, and the peel will virtually fall off.

Falling apart while cooking: (The onions, not you, of course.) Mark an *X* on the root end of the onion with a sharp knife, and it will help hold loose onions together. (The root end is usually flatter, and it has a little dark spot where the root was.)

Sautéing unevenly: You have a recipe that calls for browned onions, but as you brown them, some are dark brown while others are still white. Sprinkle the onions with a bit of sugar as they cook, and they should sauté evenly thereafter.

Smelly: Spicy smells tend to overcome oniony smells. The simplest spicy smell maker is a few cloves simmering in a pan of vinegar.

Too soft: Boiled onions that have become too soft can be firmed up again by dipping them briefly in ice water.

Wilting: When green onions start wilting, you can revive them by replanting them! Simply stick the root end in the ground, and it will take root and grow healthy again. This does not work, alas, with most other things, including human beings.

ORANGES

Bland: Vanilla is delightfully compatible with orange flavor, as the Dreamsicle people learned years ago. Add a tiny bit of vanilla extract to your indifferently flavored oranges, or to indifferently flavored orange juice as well.

Difficult to peel: Pour boiling water over the oranges and let them stand for 5 minutes. The peels will come off very easily, and so will all the white stuff under the peel. The peel is permanently loosened by this technique, so you can do it in advance and still refrigerate the oranges. This process also tends to make the oranges considerably juicier.

Unjuicy: See **ORANGES, Difficult to peel.** Or roll the oranges around on a table, as if you were trying to make them rounder. That really loosens up the old juices.

OYSTER PLANT: *see* SALSIFY

OYSTERS: *see also* CLAMS

Sandy: Sprinkle them with lots of cornmeal. Cover with cold water. Let stand for about 3 hours, then rinse well.

P

PANCAKES

Cold and soggy: Pancakes can be reheated without overcooking by placing them between the folds of a dish towel in a 250° oven.

Left over: There isn't a whole lot you can do with leftover pancakes. The Scots, however, consider them just a kind of soft crumpet to be served with butter and jam for tea. You might do the same. Or you could make sandwiches (how about with cream cheese softened with fruit juice). One cookbook suggests cutting them in strips and using them as you would use noodles. Hmm. Or perhaps you could sail them around the backyard as Frisbees.

Stuck to the griddle: Usually this means they aren't fatty enough. Next batch, add a little more shortening.

PANS: *see* Appendix H: PROBLEMS WITH UTENSILS AND APPLIANCES

PARSLEY

Difficult to chop: Wash it very briefly in hot water and dry it off with paper towels. Its chopability quotient should rise noticeably. Also, don't forget that very handy kitchen implement called the scissors.

PASTA

Boiling over: The immediate remedy is to blow on the surface of the water. This will give you about 15 seconds' grace period to look frantically around for the pot holder. If you can't find it, blow again. And again. Then put a bit of oil (about 1 tablespoon) in the water. Next time, lightly grease the top inch of the inside of the pot.

Stuck together: After pasta is drained and is stuck together, you can unstick it by plunging it quickly back into boiling water. This time, put a healthy glug of olive oil or some butter in the water. Next time, put the oil in at the start and the problem won't arise. (If pasta is permanently stuck—this can happen with lasagna noodles, for instance—slice the mass thin to make new noodles and use as you had planned, or fry the new noodles with a butter and oil mixture and some onions; use the same sauce you had originally planned.)

PASTRY

Edges browning too fast: Cover just the edges with a thin strip of aluminum foil, shaped to fit.

Too crumbly to roll: Lightly gather it together on the pastry board; cover it with a slightly dampened cloth, and let it rest for 10 minutes; then try again.

Too much: Cooked pastry can be frozen, thus providing a head start on your next pie or casserole. Microwave is perfect for reheating.

PEA SOUP: *see* SOUPS

PEACHES

Darkening: Sprinkle them with lemon juice after peeling to retard the approaching darkness.

Difficult to peel: Firm peaches can be peeled just like potatoes, using a potato peeler, which may then be called a peach peeler. Soft peaches can be peeled like tomatoes by soaking them in boiling water, off the stove, for about 3 minutes. The peel should then come off quite easily.

Fuzzy: Say, do you remember those television commercials where they used to shave a peach? (They were selling electric razors, not bald peaches.) If your peach is very ripe and very fuzzy, that may be your only solution. (Does anyone know how to get peach fuzz out of an electric-razor mechanism?) For less ripe peaches, scrub them with a vegetable brush, and they will ripen into clean-shaven peaches.

Or you can microwave a peach on high setting for 10 seconds and let it stand for 5 minutes before peeling.

Unripe: Store them in a closed paper bag for 1 or 2 days.

PEANUT BUTTER

Separating: Turn the jar upside down and put it back on the shelf.

Too thick: Peanut butter can be thinned with one of these four peanut butter thinners: soft butter, maple syrup, hot water, or orange juice. Or you can freeze the bread first, either if the sandwich isn't going to be eaten until late or if you happen to like frozen peanut butter sandwiches.

PEARS

Ripening too fast: Refrigerate them. The colder they are, the slower they will ripen.

Ripening too slow: Store them in a closed paper bag for 1 or 2 days to accelerate ripening.

PEAS

Bland: All five of the following seasonings are said to pep up tired old peas: basil, marjoram, poppy seed, rosemary, and sage. Or combine peas with minced onions that have been browned in butter. (You may call this dish Peas Lyonnaise.)

Frozen to the box: Run cold tap water into the spaces in the box, and the peas should come rolling out.

Thawed: See Appendix B to help you decide what to do about peas that have thawed out too soon.

Uncertain quality: Drop dried peas in water. The bad ones will float and the good ones will sink to the bottom.

PECANS: *see* NUTS

PEPPER: *see* HERBS, SPICES, SEASONINGS

PEPPER, GREEN: *see* GREEN PEPPERS

PERSIMMONS

Too Many: Make this delightfully simple dessert:

CINDY FRANK'S PERSIMMON SHERBET

Peel the persimmons and remove the seeds (unless you have the seedless kind, in which case don't remove the seeds). Freeze the persimmon meat. When it is frozen, put it in a food processor it and process until it is mushy. Eat.

Unripe: Here is an astonishing method for overnight ripening of unripe persimmons. The only reason it didn't make page-one headlines is that so few newspaper editors like persimmons. Wrap the unripe persimmon in aluminum foil. Put it in the freezer. When it is frozen solid, remove it and allow it to thaw at room temperature. When it is thawed out, it will be ripe. Stop the presses!

PICKLES

Not pickled enough: Put them back in the jar with a bunch of dill, unless there already is dill in the jar. The longer they sit, the more pickled they get, until eventually they may burn a hole right through the jar.

Scum on jar: Float 1 teaspoon of olive oil on the surface of the liquid in the jar, and the scum will go away and not return.

PIES: *see also* CAKE; COOKIES; CREAM PUFFS; PASTRY

Bland: Ground allspice is a fine pepper-upper for most kinds of pies, including apple, berry, raisin, pumpkin, prune, and custard, among others. Add ¼ teaspoon to the filling, to start with.

Caraway seeds in the crust give apple pie a different and interesting taste. Add 1 teaspoon per 2 cups of flour. Two other good things to add: cumin to the fruit of a fruit pie before putting on the top crust; fennel sprinkled on top of the crust before baking.

Drying out while cooking: Erecting a small smokestack in the center of the pie permits the heat to escape, so it doesn't stay inside and boil the juices away. The simplest sort of smokestack is a piece of raw macaroni inserted vertically, right in the middle of the pie.

If the pie has already dried out too much, you can wet it by making a simple syrup (see following recipes), adding a dash of rum or cognac if it suits your fancy, and pouring it through the slashes in the crust.

SIMPLE SYRUP

½ cup sugar
1 cup water

Put the sugar in the water, in a saucepan. Cover. Bring to a boil. Uncover. Simmer 3 minutes. Store leftover in the refrigerator.

SIMPLER SYRUP

¼ cup currant jelly
½ cup water

Stir them together and heat to boiling.

SIMPLEST SYRUP

syrup

Use maple syrup right from the bottle.

Hot: The traditional way of cooling pies is to put them on the windowsill, from which they will be stolen by cute freckle-faced boys. Now that the windowsill is going the way of the running board, pies may be cooled quickly by putting a layer of ice cubes in a big pan and resting the pie tin on top of the ice cubes.

Not enough filling: Shorten the side crust to the top of the filling and serve it as a flan or as a tart with a lattice crust.

Soggy crust: Brush the sides and the top crust with a beaten (but not fluffy) egg white, and put in a hot (400°) oven for 4 minutes.

Too sweet: Add the juice of half a lemon to the filling. This also helps to bring out the flavor of the fruit, especially in berry pies.

PINEAPPLE

Canned flavor: Soak the pineapple slices or chunks in cold water for half an hour to take away their "tin can" taste.

Difficult to peel: It can be difficult if you don't have one of those $3-billion machines they use in pineapple factories. So how about slicing the pineapple first and then cutting away the peel and the core afterward. Much easier.

Unripe: Speed up the ripening process by sealing the pineapple in a brown paper bag and storing it in a warm (not hot) place. You'll know it's ripe when one of the center leaves pulls out easily.

PIZZA

Burned: It is almost always the crust and not the topping that gets burned. Scrape off the topping onto another pizza, or toast if you're in a hurry, or stir into a macaroni casserole.

Too gunky to cut: Sometimes pizzas are so gunky that even those circular pizza knives don't work effectively. In such cases, try cutting the pizza apart with ordinary kitchen scissors. (You can even use out-of-the-ordinary kitchen scissors, if that's what you have.)

PLATES: *see* Appendix H: PROBLEMS WITH UTENSILS AND APPLIANCES

POPCORN

Won't pop: The usual reason is that it is too dry. Soak the kernels in water for 5 minutes, drain them, and try again.

If this doesn't work, an almost certain remedy is to freeze the kernels for 24 hours or more and pop them while they are still frozen. (Some people store their popcorn in the freezer for this reason.)

PORK

Bland: These seasonings go best with pork: caraway seeds, cardamom (about 1 teaspoon per 4 servings), chervil, cloves (four or five in the marinade), coriander, cumin, fennel (put ½ teaspoon into a roast), juniper berries, marjoram, oregano (mix and rub on a roast), paprika, rosemary, and sage.

Salty: If salt pork is too salty, blanch it: Drop it into water that is just simmering for 2 minutes. When you remove it, plunge it into a bowl of cold water to stop it from cooking. You can do this with a chunk of salt pork or with small pieces. Lower small pieces into the water in a sieve so they'll be easier to retrieve.

POT ROAST

Fatty: If your pot roast really looks too fatty to be acceptable, cook it well, chill it in the refrigerator, remove the now-solidified fat, and return it to the pot, or wherever it was.

Tough: In addition to the usual meat tenderizers, you might consider adding tomatoes to the pot the roast is roasting in. The acid in tomatoes breaks down the fibers in the meat, thereby tenderizing same.

If you don't have 3 hours to simmer the roast, slice it very thin, put it back in the pot for 15 minutes, and then serve.

POTATOES

Baked—cold: Baked potatoes can be reheated without overcooking by dipping them in cold water, then putting them into a 350° oven for 10 minutes.

Baked—exploding: This time, duck! Next time, cut a slice in the potato, or puncture it to let the steam escape, thereby preventing explosions.

Baked—fast method: Parboiling for 5 minutes before baking, or sticking one of those potato nails (or any big aluminum nail) through the potato will cut the baking time by about 20 minutes. For faster baked potatoes, wrap them tightly in foil, put them on a rack, and cook them for 15 minutes. Of course some people consider the 5-minute baked potato sufficient reason for owning a microwave oven.

Boiled—bland: Add a pinch of rosemary or a bay leaf to the cooking liquid. Or top them with sour cream to which you have added a pinch of marjoram.

Boiled—disintegrating: Oh, and you were making them for the picnic potato salad. . . . Use extra crunchy bits like celery, chopped green onions, and dill pickle. Combine everything you can and add it to the potatoes. Toss lightly and then spoon into a bowl or mold and firm it down. Chill. Turn it out and decorate with parsley. A triumph from a disaster.

Boiled—old and stale: Add a slice of lemon to the water. It tends to prevent discoloring and helps bring out what flavor remains.

Boiled—skin sticks to knife or hands while peeling: Dab a tiny bit of butter or other shortening on the knife, peeler, and/or hands, whichever it is that is troubled by sticky peels.

Mashed—bland or too much: There comes a time in everyone's life, often at an early age, when he or she just can't stomach another spoonful of mashed potatoes. If you have just made a large batch when this phenomenon comes suddenly upon your family, try adding some nutmeg to the potatoes and frying, as patties, in butter. Not bad at all.

Mashed—won't fluff: Add a pinch or two of baking powder to the potatoes, and keep on fluffing.

Not enough: But why don't you have mashed-potato flakes, as we suggested in the Introduction? But enough of that. If you haven't started cooking the potatoes you do have, slice them thin and make scalloped potatoes or Potatoes Anna (they're richer so people will eat less; check your cookbook for details). They will be fully cooked in 45 minutes at 300°—a bit faster at higher temperatures or with smaller potatoes, or with ones you've cut in half.

POTATO CHIPS

Broken: Here is something mildly interesting to do with broken potato chips—more interesting than throwing them out, and faster than gluing them back together with Crazy Glue: Break them up even more and use them as a casserole topping.

Soggy: Put them very briefly under the broiler; don't let them brown. Or you can microwave them for 30 to 60 seconds on the high setting, and let them stand for 3 minutes.

POULTRY

Bland: Try rubbing the bird with marjoram (which is also interesting in chicken salad). Mix oregano with olive oil, and rub it on the fowl. Likewise with rosemary or tarragon or thyme. Mix some hot mustard, oregano, paprika, or sesame seed in with the batter for fried chicken. Crush three or four juniper berries into the chicken salad. And so on.

Breading falls off: *see* **BREADING, Falls off**

Difficult to cut: Often scissors are easier to use for cooked or raw birds. With cooked chicken or turkey, it doesn't shred the meat as much as a knife.

Dry: Turkey, in particular, can get so dry it makes your tongue fuzzy. Slice the turkey and arrange it on a heatproof platter. Make a sauce of half butter and half chicken broth. Pour it on the sliced bird, and let it stand in a 250° oven for 10 minutes to soak up the juices.

Feathery: In our modern age of convenience, most birds come defeathered. In our modern age of deteriorating personal services, often the defeathering isn't good enough. If you don't have a chicken plucker on your household staff, here are two reasonably simple methods of defeathering a fowl:

1. The hot wax treatment: Add paraffin or old candles to boiling water. Wait until the wax melts. Dip the bird up and down in the pot until it is coated with wax. Wrap in newspapers and cool. Now, as you peel off the wax, the feathers should come off along with it. (If you can't get the wax off, stick a wick in the bird's beak and you have an emergency candle.)[Ed. note: Is this a joke?][Author note: Yes.]

2. The soap method: Heat a big pot of water to boiling. Add ¼ cup dishwasher detergent. Drop the fowl in the water, slosh it around for 2 or 3 minutes, and roll it up in a towel. You should be able to rub off any remaining feathers. Follow with a cool-water rinse, and don't worry about the taste: no soap.

Freezer burn: Dry spots on frozen fowl can and usually do mean freezer burn. Smell the creature carefully, and if you have any doubts as to its condition, return it or junk it. If it smells all right, rub the skin with oil just before roasting.

Frozen: Manufacturers usually recommend that frozen chickens and turkeys be defrosted slowly in the refrigerator—a process that often takes 3 or 4 days. The main reason for this recommendation is that faster thawing causes the bird to lose juices and thus become tougher. You can overcome this to some extent by thawing your bird in an airtight place, like a big plastic bag. If you're in a hurry, put the bag in a bowl of lukewarm water.

Gamey: Sometimes duck or pheasant or even turkey will taste too gamey for your palate. This is no reflection on the bird's behavior in the barnyard. Ginger, sherry, and brandy (the latter two applied to the bird, please) have a tendency to lessen gamey taste in poultry. You can rub ½ teaspoon of powdered ginger into the bird's skin before roasting or add any of the three to the gravy or sauce you serve over the meat.

Not enough: Serve the poultry on a waffle that you have made by adding 2 teaspoons of poultry seasoning to the batter before adding the liquid. You can get away with about half as much meat this way.

Pale: Paprika, applied liberally to the skin of a fowl before roasting it, will ensure a rich color. You can sprinkle it on at any point in the cooking process to help a pallid bird.

Tough: Meat tenderizer will work on fowl as well. For poultry cooked in liquid, try adding a pinch of baking soda to the liquid. And for broiling or roasting, tenderize the birds by rubbing them inside and out with lemon juice before cooking.

PRUNES

Bland: Add thin lemon slices while cooking cooked prunes.

Dry, tough: Cover them with boiling water. Put in the refrigerator overnight. This doesn't cook them; it just plumps them nicely up. You can do this quickly in a microwave oven. Cover a layer of prunes with water, add a squeeze of lemon juice if you wish, and cook on high for 5 minutes. Let stand for 5 minutes, and either eat or refrigerate in the liquid.

PUDDINGS AND CUSTARDS

Bland: Toss a bay leaf or a pinch of ginger into almost any kind of custard. Bland puddings can benefit from the addition of ground allspice, cinnamon, ginger, mace (especially in chocolate), and nutmeg.

Cold: Hot puddings and custards can be reheated without cooking them more by covering them with lettuce leaves and returning to a warm oven until you are ready for them.

Curdling: When pudding starts to curdle, the first thing to do is to stop it from cooking any further. Do this by hastily putting the pan in cold water—better still, ice water. (This may be the origin of the Hastily Putting Club.) Then beat it with an eggbeater or whisk until it is smooth again.

If the pudding or, especially, custard has already curdled, you can frequently uncurdle it with this time-consuming method: Add 1 tablespoon of custard to 1 teaspoon of milk or liqueur. Beat until creamy. Add the remaining custard 1 tablespoon at a time, beating each time until creamy. Then return to your recipe.

Separating: This is caused by too high heat. The oven should be at 325°, and the custard should be in Marie's bath (that is to say, a bain-marie: the custard dish standing in a pan of water).

Skin is forming: If the taste is compatible, sprinkle 1 teaspoon of sugar on the surface. If it is not, put wax paper on the surface, and remove it when the pudding has cooled.

Too thin: For creamy puddings that are too thin, add any (not all) of the following for each cup of milk used: 3 tablespoons flour or 1 tablespoon cornstarch or 1½ tablespoons rice flour or 1 tablespoon arrowroot or 1 tablespoon tapioca. (Mix the thickeners with a little cold milk before adding.)

For molded puddings, add any of the following for each cup of milk used: 4 tablespoons flour or 1½ tablespoons cornstarch or 2½ tablespoons cornmeal or 2 tablespoons rice flour. (Mix the thickeners with a little cold milk before adding.)

For soft custard: add one egg (or two yolks or two whites) for each cup of milk.

For molded custard: double the quantity of eggs or use ½ tablespoon gelatin powder per cup of milk.

PUFF PASTRY

Doesn't rise: Slice off the top and bottom. Scrape the soggy bits from the middle. (You may wish to spread them in a pan and bake them to make great crumbs.) If the bottom isn't burned, use it; if it is, discard it. Use the top as a lid on whatever you were going to put in the middle. If the middle is soft, use a bowl; if it isn't, use a plate.

PUMPKIN: see SQUASH, SWEET POTATOES, PUMPKIN

PUNCH: see ALCOHOL

QUICHE

Soggy crust: The main cause is using wet vegetables—either undrained, or moisture-holding (like cooked zucchini). Remove the portion above the crust and serve that alone. Most people either (1) won't notice, (2) will be too polite to comment, or (3) will assume it was intentional. Yes, if you have time, you can bake a round of crust and put the quiche-middle on it. Scallop the edges so it looks intentional. How do you get the quiche out of the pan and onto the crust? Loosen it around the edge with a sharp knife. Put plastic wrap on the top of the cooled quiche. Put a terry-cloth towel over that. Put a plate over that. Turn it upside down. Hope.

RADISHES

Wilted, soft, soggy: Soak them in ice water for 2 to 3 hours. Option: Add 1 tablespoon of vinegar or the juice of one lemon to the water.

RAGOUT: *see* STEW

RAISINS

Shriveled: You can replumpify shriveled raisins by simmering them in just enough water to cover them, for 3 to 4 minutes. Or put a thin layer in a dish, just covering them with water, and cook them on high in a microwave for 5 minutes. Let stand an additional 5 minutes. Use part rum or sherry if you wish. But wait, aren't raisins *supposed* to be shriveled, though? Oh, well.

Sink to the bottom: If raisins are sinking to the bottom of your cakes or cookies or whatever, coat them lightly with flour and they will disperse themselves throughout the whatever, just the way you wanted. If what you are making is raisin upside-down cake, ignore this.

Stuck together: Heat your congealed mass of raisins in the oven at 300° for a few minutes, and they will unstick themselves.

RAREBIT, WELSH: *see* CHEESE, Cooked cheese that is rubbery, tough, stringy

RASPBERRIES: *see* BERRIES

RAVIOLI: *see* PASTA

RHUBARB

Too tart: All rhubarb is too tart, some of us think. To de-tart it without adding absurd amounts of sugar, cut up the rhubarb and soak it for 3 minutes in hot water to which you have added a pinch of either baking soda or salt.

RICE

Boiling over: First, blow on the surface of the water. This will cool the water down enough so that it will stop boiling over. For a longer-term preventive, toss a lump of butter in the pot; it will flavor the rice pleasantly as well.

Burned: As soon as you discover you've burned the rice again, turn off the flame, place the heel of a loaf of bread on top of the rice, cover the pot, and wait 5 minutes. Virtually all the scorched taste should disappear into the bread. Serve the rice to friends and the bread to enemies.

Cold: Reheat rice without overcooking by putting it in either a big sieve or a colander and placing it over a pan of boiling or simmering water (depending on how cold it is and how fast you need it). Keep the rice from touching the water.

Not white enough: Are you sure it isn't brown rice? All right, just asking. Add 1 teaspoon of lemon juice to the cooking water, and the rice will whiten.

Too much: You can reheat leftover rice (see **RICE, Cold**), add it to soup, use it as a casserole ingredient, or combine with custard to make a rice pudding. Or you could make something unusual, like:

RICE FRITTERS

½ package dry yeast
½ cup very warm (about 110°) water
1½ to 2 cups leftover lukewarm rice
3 eggs, beaten
1 cup all-purpose flour
¼ cup sugar
½ teaspoon salt
¼ teaspoon cinnamon
Confectioners' sugar
Whipped cream

Dissolve the yeast in the water. Mix in the rice. Cover and let sit overnight in the refrigerator. Next day, add the eggs, flour, sugar, salt, and cinnamon, stir well, and let it sit for another hour or so, this time at room temperature. Drop this mixture one teaspoonful at a time into hot deep fat (360°) and fry until golden brown. Serve as an accompaniment to ham or chicken, or sprinkle with confectioners' sugar and serve with whipped cream, for a dessert.

Uneven cooking: When rice at the bottom of the pot is cooked and the top of the pot is raw, it means too much steam is escaping. Give the rice a big stir, cover the pot either with foil or with a Turkish towel (be sure to fold the loose ends up over the top), replace the lid, and keep right on cooking.

ROAST BEEF

Difficult to carve: Let the roast sit for 15 minutes out of the oven. The juices will "set," and the roast will be less likely to fall apart as you carve it.

Not browning: Steam impedes browning. If it is covered, there will be more steam, so uncover it. It is generally best to roast a roast in a shallow uncovered pan.

Not enough: Slice the beef thinly, serve it over toast, and cover with a sauce. You can use cheese soup as a sauce if you like meat-and-cheese dinners; tomato sauce made from a can of tomato soup (see the recipe on the label, or in your big cookbook); hollandaise (you *have* completed your "first aid" kit by now, haven't you?); or add a pinch of tarragon to the hollandaise and you have béarnaise sauce.

Overcooked: Cut off all unusable burned pieces, and slice the roast thinly. It will probably be dry and tough, in which case you can float it in a sauce (see **ROAST BEEF, Not enough**).

Too rare: Often the outside slices of a roast are acceptable when the middle section is too rare for some people, misguided as they may be. Serve the outer slices and return the rest to cook while you eat the first helpings, or broil the too-rare slices to desired doneness.

Too tough: Unfortunately, this is usually discovered at the dinner table, when all you can do is slice it very thin. But you'll probably have leftovers. The good news is that meat cooked by a dry method (roasting, broiling, etc.) can be tenderized by a moist-heat method for its second appearance. Braising and stewing, which use low heat for a long cooking time, are best. Consider, then, resurrecting your roast as an impressive Beef Burgundy.

ROLLS: *see* BREAD AND ROLLS

RUM: *see* ALCOHOL

RUTABAGAS

Smelly: A recent national survey showed that .0000000001 percent of the population was troubled by smelly rutabagas. For you, madam or sir, this advice: add 1 teaspoon of sugar to the cooking water.

SALAD: *see* GREENS

SALAD DRESSING: *see also* SAUCES

Bland: One interesting way to pep up bottled store-bought French or Italian dressing is to put a halved clove of garlic in the bottle and let it stand overnight or longer.

SALSIFY

Darkening: The same person who has smelly rutabagas also has darkening salsify. Store this herb in water to which you have added 2 tablespoons of vinegar or the juice of 1 lemon for each quart of water.

SALT: *see* HERBS, SPICES, SEASONINGS

SALT PORK: *see* PORK

SANDWICHES: *see* BREAD AND ROLLS; MUFFINS; *specific sandwich ingredients*

SAUCES

Bitter: A common cause of unexpectedly bitter sauce is tomato seeds. This time, strain them out as best you can. (Then, if necessary, see **SAUCES, Too thin.**) Next time, see **TOMATOES, Seedy.**

Bland: Every herb, spice, seasoning, bottled flavoring, and kind of cooking alcohol in your house can be used in sauces. There is no excuse whatever for a flat or bland sauce. Consult your favorite cookbook and get to work. (If you are reducing a sauce, add seasonings at the end, or you may overdo it, since the herbs don't reduce.) If you absolutely can't think of anything else to do, add a dollop of sherry to any sauce whatsoever, and at least people will know you tried. On page xv, under "Hollandaise sauce (cans or packages)," you will find simple instructions for converting this store-bought ready-to-use product into quick béarnaise, choron, and maltaise sauces.

Catsup: *see* **Ketchup** in this section

Curdled: Remove sauce from the heat at once. For delicate sauces, like hollandaise, add an ice cube to retard further cooking. Beat hard with a hand beater or whisk (having removed the ice cube). If necessary, strain the sauce too. For other sauces, try adding a little cream, then continue cooking. Next time use a double boiler or lower heat, stir constantly, and add the fragile curdle-producing ingredients (usually eggs, cream, sour cream—at room temperature) just before serving. Also pay attention to the weather. Sauces are more likely to curdle in humid weather, perhaps especially during thunderstorms.

Fatty: Chill, skim off the fat, and reheat. For fast skimming, take off as much fat as you can with a spoon (it's easier if you tilt the pot). Then toss in a few ice cubes, wait until the fat congeals on them, and remove them. Blot the last bits up with paper towels laid on the surface of the sauce and reheat.

Consider a sauce boat or pitcher in which the spout goes to the bottom, so you are pouring the least fatty sauce directly from the bottom. Most gourmet or kitchen stores have such things.

Ketchup won't pour: Put a soda straw down to the bottom of the bottle. It will transmit enough air down to the bottom to permit the ketchup to pour readily.

Lumpy: If you can, push the sauce through a strainer. If you can't, beat it with a whisk or hand beater. Use electric appliances (beater, blender, food processor) only as a last resort.

Not enough: Whether your problem is too little liquid in a stew or not enough gravy for a roast, the solution is basically the same: Add more liquid to what you have (though don't try to add more than an amount of liquid equal to what you started out with), re-season, decide if you can get away with a thinner sauce, and then thicken if you must. Consider using something more substantial than water for your thinning: consommé or bouillon (be careful with the salt when you re-season), liquid from a compatible cooked vegetable you're serving with the meal, or even orange juice for something like ham or poultry-based dishes. To avoid slowing everything down, have your liquid hot before adding it.

Cream sauces can be extended by adding more white sauce (you'll find medium white sauce recipes in most cookbooks) or even cream of mushroom or chicken soups if you're really strapped for time.

Hollandaise-based sauces are best left in their original, rich, unadulterated state. Put food and sauce on plates in the kitchen yourself; no one will even think to question the volume of the sauce.

Not rich enough: Add heavy cream, 1 teaspoon at a time, after all the sauce is cooked and removed from the heat. A lump of butter, applied in like manner, will also work.

Not smooth enough: A little butter stirred into a cream sauce before serving will produce a more satiny texture.

Salty: The only certain cure for saltiness is to increase the volume without adding more salt. Otherwise, you can add a couple of pinches of brown sugar. It tends to overcome saltiness without adding noticeable sweetening.

Separating: *see* **SAUCES, Curdled**

Too thin: There are almost as many thickeners as there are sauces. The universal one is time. Keep cooking until some liquid evaporates, and the sauce inevitably will thicken. (Some French recipes require sauce ingredients to be reduced by 90 percent or more. There is an account of a famous sauce whose secret recipe began "Reduce 1 ox to 1 cup.")

Cornstarch is a good thickener when translucency of sauce is desirable, as in many dessert or Chinese sauces. Add 1 tablespoon per 1½ to 2 cups of cooking liquid. To prevent lumps, dissolve the cornstarch in cold water, then add to the hot sauce.

Arrowroot: ½ tablespoon per 1½ to 2 cups, but only when the sauce will be served within 10 minutes. To prevent lumps, dissolve the arrowroot in cold water, then add to the hot sauce.

One cup of milk or a milk-based sauce will be thickened by 4 tablespoons of flour, 1 cup of bread crumbs, 3 to 4 tablespoons of tapioca, or 2 egg yolks beaten with ¼ cup of cream or evaporated milk. The latter should be done only in the top of a double boiler, stirring constantly.

Other sauce thickeners that may be appropriate for your particular sauce are rice, barley, milk, cream, and mashed-potato flakes.

SAUSAGES

Bursting, splitting, exploding, etc.: There are two schools of thought: the Low Temperaturists and the Skin Piercers. Either is likely to work; both are unnecessary. Next time, cook the sausages using just enough water to cover, and if you are using the precooked variety (many are nowadays), use hot but not boiling water.

SCALLIONS: *see* ONIONS

SEAFOOD: *see* FISH AND SEAFOOD

SEASONINGS: *see* **HERBS, SPICES, SEASONINGS**

SHORTENING: *see* **FAT, LARD, SHORTENING**

SHRIMP: *see* **FISH AND SEAFOOD**

SODA POP

Decarbonated: Cover tightly and shake well; some of the carbonation will be restored if it isn't too far gone. Open carefully; the soda may shoot across the room if you do it too fast.

Uninspired: When you have grown weary of all the usual flavors, it is fun to start experimenting with combining two kinds of soda (cherry and cola is, of course, a classic, but many others make sense too: ginger ale with orange or grape; cream soda with strawberry or cherry; cola with lemon or lime). Our family adds flavoring agents (essence of cherry, rum, almond, peppermint, and the like) to various sodas (cream soda with almond is a special favorite); and also milk does interesting things: the classic "root beer cow" (about ⅓ milk), the chocolate egg cream (no egg or cream, just cream soda, milk, and chocolate essence or syrup), and so forth.

SOUFFLÉS

Doesn't rise (or rises, then sinks): It probably still tastes as good (perhaps better; a collapsed chocolate soufflé we created in doing our research for this book was wonderfully dense and chocolatey). So, for a savory (nonsweet) soufflé, if you do wish to disguise it, remove it from the pan, cover with cheese, and broil. Call it a frittata. Or simply cover it with a sauce appropriate to the ingredients. A sweet soufflé can just be covered with whipped cream and/or an appropriate sauce.

Traditional soufflés will not rise again if reheated. Some cookbooks offer recipes for "double rising" soufflés that do, in fact, rise again when reheated. We're not using up three pages to present these, because we feel it is more a matter of the ego than the palate.

Next time, be sure to bake the soufflé on the lowest rack in the oven. This is partly because it is hotter down there (in most ovens) and partly so that, as it does rise, it won't smash into the top of the oven, quite possibly lifting the roof off your house.

Top is browning too fast: Make a foil "lid" to cover it. You'll have to guess the approximate size because you shouldn't take it out of the oven in midbaking. Cut a circle about 2 inches wider than the top of the soufflé. Bend the edges up about 1 inch in from the outside (to make a pie tin–like shape). Oil the inside lightly. Open the oven and quickly slide the foil, oiled-side down, onto the soufflé and continue baking.

Uncrowned: To make a crown, just before baking, run a knife around the mixture about 1 inch in from the edge. The tip of the knife should be near but not at the bottom of the pan.

SOUPS

Bland: Chicken extract or bouillon will beef (or chicken) up a pallid soup. Beef extract or bouillon will do the same, and so will yeast extract. Here is a list of common herbs and spices and their most exemplary uses in soups:

allspice (whole): pea, ham, vegetable, beef, and tomato soups.

basil: tomato, turtle, spinach, and minestrone (½ teaspoon per 4 servings).

bay leaf: vegetable, minestrone, and tomato.

chervil: tomato and spinach.

cumin: a dash in creamed chicken, fish, and pea.

juniper berries: three or four in 4 servings of vegetable, beef, lamb, or oxtail.

mace: one or two blades (or pinches if it's ground) in 4 cups of consommé stock.

marjoram: spinach, clam, turtle, and onion (½ teaspoon per 4 servings).

oregano: tomato, bean, corn, and pea (add 5 minutes before serving).

rosemary: chicken, pea, spinach, potato, and fish.

sage: creamed soups and chowders.

savory: fish, consommé, lentil, bean, tomato, and vegetable.

sesame seed: creamed soups (sprinkle on before serving).

tarragon: tomato, vegetable, and seafood.

thyme: chicken, onion, potato, tomato, and seafood soups; gumbo; borscht (stir in ½ teaspoon 10 minutes before serving).

Consider leaving the soup alone and putting something interesting in the bowls. Flavored croutons, a dollop of sour cream or crème fraîche (see **CRÉME FRAÎCHE**), swirls of tomato paste, sherry, curry powder. See also **SOUPS, Not enough**.

Bouillon cloudy: Add eggshells. Please remove them before serving. Or add egg whites. To remove them (if you want to), strain through a cheesecloth-lined strainer or colander.

Cold: Reheat thin soups in a heavy skillet over a very low heat just to the boiling point.

Reheat thick soups in a deep casserole in a 375° oven until hot, stirring occasionally.

Consommé won't jell: This happens most often to canned consommé that has been around for a long time. The general rule for any consommé is that 1 tablespoon of gelatin powder (dissolved first in 2 tablespoons of hot consommé) will solidify 2 cups of consommé.

Fatty or greasy: If you have the time, refrigerate the soup. The fat will solidify on the top. Remove it and reheat (see **SOUPS, Cold**).

If you don't have the time, you can slurp up the fat from the top with a baster, or you can float a grease collector on the top. Lettuce leaves, blotting paper, and paper towels all make good grease collectors.

Another fast technique is to make a "grease magnet" by wrapping a few ice cubes in a terry-cloth towel. Run this over the top of the soup, and the fat will cling to it. A ladle full of ice cubes will have the same effect.

Light: There are commercial soup colorings, but some people think they have a telltale aroma. Depending on the kind of soup, you can darken it either with tomato skins or with a mixture (for each 2 quarts of soup) of 1 teaspoon of ground cinnamon, ½ teaspoon of cloves and ¼ teaspoon of allspice dissolved in a cup of soup and added just before serving.

You can also try adding a tablespoon of caramelized sugar. This works well with soups that feature cabbage. If you think you've overdone it and can detect a sweet taste, add a tablespoon or two of vinegar. The result will be a much more complex and interestingly flavored soup.

Not enough: Rather than add more liquid, consider making it spicier, thus servable in smaller portions. For example, hot or taco sauce in tomato- or chicken-based soups; aioli (garlic mayonnaise) in fishy soups; curry powder in many soups. Also consider making it richer, for the same smaller-portions reasons: add, for instance, a roux and thick cream.

Salty: The surest solution is to increase the quantity of liquid without increasing the quantity of salt. But if this isn't practical, try one of the following three techniques:

1. Tomatoes. If it is the right kind of soup, add a can of tomatoes. They are sufficiently bland to use up a lot of the saltiness.

2. A few pinches of brown sugar. It won't de-salt the soup, but it may help cover up the salty taste without sweetening the soup.

3. Potatoes. Add a thin-sliced raw potato, and keep it in the soup until the slices become translucent; they may absorb some of the salt from the liquid.

There are skeptics who ask, "If it is possible to remove salt from liquid easily, why aren't we de-salting the oceans?" To this we reply, "Because it would require 488,391,000,000,000 tons of sliced potatoes."

Too much: Contrary to almost everyone else's opinion, leftover soup can be kept almost indefinitely without freezing it, if you're willing to work at it. Almost any soup will keep in a covered pot in the refrigerator for a week. If you have a great soup that you want to keep longer but don't want to freeze, take it out of the refrigerator and heat it to boiling every couple of days, and it can last for a year.

Too thin: First see the section on **SAUCES, Too thin** for several useful hints. Thickeners peculiar to soups include these:

Mashed potatoes or potato flakes (which also have a tendency to absorb seasonings, so check for taste after adding).

Some of the soup's own ingredients (e.g., meat, vegetables) ground up in a blender or food processor. (These should be additional ingredients, but in a pinch may be filched from the soup.)

A mixture of ½ cup cornstarch and ¼ cup sherry, stirred in shortly before serving.

One teaspoon of barley or rice or 2 teaspoons of flour (first dissolved in enough cold water to make a runny mixture, then stirred into the soup) for each original cup of liquid, stirred in during the last hour of cooking.

One egg yolk beaten with 1 tablespoon of cream of sherry, mixed with a small amount of hot soup, and then stirred into the rest just before serving.

Stale bread (especially if you can float a heaping tablespoon of Parmesan cheese on top, too).

For long-cooking soups, a handful of oatmeal or barley flakes.

For pea and bean soups, 1 teaspoon of vinegar. (It will thicken without affecting the taste.)

SOUP STOCK

Have none, need some: Two bouillon cubes (beef or chicken) in a cup of water make an acceptable substitute for beef or chicken stock. Watch your salt levels, since bouillon is saltier than stock.

SOUR CREAM

Have none, need some: For cooking purposes, not topping purposes, add 1 tablespoon of mild vinegar or lemon juice to 1 cup of evaporated milk.

For topping purposes, not cooking purposes, put cottage cheese in a blender or food processor, sweeten it to taste, and if it doesn't taste right, add a tiny bit of vanilla extract.

Or make crème fraîche (see, surprisingly, **CRÈME FRAÎCHE**).

SPAGHETTI: *see* PASTA

SPAGHETTI SAUCE: *see* SAUCES

SPICES: *see* HERBS, SPICES, SEASONINGS

SPINACH: *see* GREENS

SQUASH, SWEET POTATOES, PUMPKIN

Bland: Squash, unbeknownst to many gastronomes, has a luscious affinity for ginger. To demonstrate this to yourself, serve squash of almost any sort with a heaping tablespoon of ginger marmalade per serving.

If this doesn't suit your fancy, try basil, ground cloves, dill seed, dill weed, mace, marjoram, oregano, sage, and thyme.

Difficult to cut: Winter squash can be rock hard. To make cutting squash easier, place it on the floor of a microwave oven and heat on high for 2 minutes. Let it stand 2 minutes before cutting.

Not enough: The orange-colored squashes go well with fruits, so combine chunks, or even purées, of them with sautéed apples or pears or sections of mandarin or regular oranges.

Green and yellow squashes love tomatoes.

Stringy: Beat stringy squash with an electric mixer at high speed for 10 seconds, then at low speed for 60 seconds. Wash the strings off the beater (the floor, the walls, the dog), and repeat if necessary and possible.

Too much: Squash keeps better than almost any other vegetable, so don't worry.

STEAK

Breading falls off: If this is your problem with chicken-fried steak, see **BREADING, Falls off**.

Curling: Cut through the fat along the edge of meat every inch or so, and turn it over. You can turn it back again later.

Overdone: Continue cooking it until it is completely charred and use it to scratch pictures on the walls of your cave. Or, perhaps more real-istically, how about covering your mistake (and the steak) with:

JOE'S HOT SAUCE

For about 2 pounds of steak

2/3 cup chopped onions
1/3 cup chopped green peppers
2 tablespoons olive oil
2/3 cup diced tomatoes
1 teaspoon salt
1/8 teaspoon chile peppers
2/3 teaspoon paprika
2/3 cup ground peanuts
1 cup chicken broth
1/4 cup sour or heavy cream

Sauté onions and peppers in olive oil for 5 minutes. Add tomatoes, salt, chile peppers, and paprika and sauté for 5 minutes more. Mix in peanuts and broth and simmer for 30 minutes. Stir in cream, pour over steak, and serve.

Tough: If you don't have, or would rather not use tenderizer, and if perforating the steak with a fork every 1/4 inch doesn't appeal, try pounding it all over with the edge of a metal pie plate. Very effective, especially if you remove the pie first.

STEW

Bland: No stew has been made that couldn't be perked up by adding 4 tablespoons of sherry and stirring well just before serving. (If you think you've made one that couldn't be so improved, we'd like to see it. Smear some on a postcard and send it on in.)

Burned: Transfer the unstuck part, without scraping any of the stuck part, to another pot at once. A wooden spoon is best. Add more water if necessary. Add some more onions; they tend to overcome any of the burned flavor that may remain.

Falling apart: Sometimes stew just cooks itself to bits. You can't reassemble it, so serve it over noodles or rice; it will look like a great sauce.

Fatty: If the consistency permits, the fat may be skimmed off with a paper towel.

If it doesn't, chill the stew after it is fully cooked (you can put it in the freezer for a while). Then remove the solidified fat. Most stews taste better the next day anyway.

Not enough: Serve the stew over noodles. Add more vegetables—and don't forget that beans are protein food. A can of kidney or Lima beans can stretch a stew without thinning it out.

Salty: Increase the quantity without adding more salt if at all possible. If not, add a couple of pinches of brown sugar; it tends to mask the saltiness without adding any noticeable sweetness.

Too thin: The best thickener for most stews is a handful of mashed potato flakes stirred in. See also **SOUPS, Too thin**, for additional suggestions.

Tough: This usually means you haven't cooked it long enough. How much time have you? You can fish the chunks of meat out and cut them smaller, in addition to the following: A teaspoon of sugar in the stewpot will help make tough stew meat grow tender much faster. The acid in tomatoes has the same effect, so add some fresh or canned tomatoes if they will be compatible.

Turning grey: When you're browning the meat at the start and instead of brown it's turning grey, the problem is too much moisture in the pan, causing steam, which causes greyness. This time, try to cut down on overcrowding, either by removing some meat or using a larger pan. Next time, be sure the meat is very dry before browning.

STOCK: *see* **SOUPS**

STRAWBERRIES: *see* **BERRIES**

STRING BEANS: *see* **BEANS, LIMA AND STRING**

STUFFING

Bland: Add allspice, basil, a crushed bay leaf, coriander, ginger, marjoram, oregano, sage, savory, and/or thyme.

Or perhaps the stuffing could use diced celery, chopped chestnuts or walnuts, diced onions (browned or not), or sauce, or bacon, browned and crumbled in.

SUGAR

Hard, lumpy, solidified: Here are seven things to do with hardened or lumpy sugar—the least drastic first, and so on, up to the last resort.

1. Push it through a sieve.

2. Roll it out with a rolling pin.

3. Steam it in the top of a double boiler.

4. Put it, in its bag (but not box) in a 350° oven. By the time the bag is warm, the sugar should be softened or delumped.

5. Put it through a food processor, blender, or meat grinder.

6. Put a wedge of apple into the box or bag of sugar and reclose it. Microwave it on high for 20 seconds per cup of sugar. Let it stand for 5 minutes. Repeat if necessary.

7. Give up and melt it down over slow heat on the stove. It makes good syrup. Add extracts, such as vanilla, maple, or butterscotch.

To keep sugar from going hard or lumpy in the future, especially brown sugar, keep it in an airtight jar, preferably in the refrigerator. To be doubly sure, keep a piece of apple or lemon in the jar.

Have none, need some: In cooking, the following may be substituted for 1 cup of sugar (and don't forget to reduce the amount of other liquids in the recipe where appropriate): ¾ cup honey, 1½ cups molasses, 2 cups corn syrup, or 1½ cups maple syrup.

Also bear in mind that you can make superfine sugar out of regular granulated sugar, in your blender or food processor.

SWEET POTATOES: *see* SQUASH, SWEET POTATOES, PUMPKIN

SWISS CHARD: *see* GREENS

SYRUP

Crystallized: Heat it gently, and the crystals should go away. Probably the simplest way is by standing the syrup jug or bottle in a large bowl of hot water. Alternatively, heat the syrup for 90 seconds per cup on a high setting in a microwave oven.

TEA

Cloudy: For hot tea, put a couple of lemon slices in the pitcher or pot. For iced tea, add a small dash of boiling water.

TOMATOES

Acidy: Canned tomatoes sometimes get unpleasantly acidic in taste. Add 1 teaspoon of sugar to a 2-pound-or-so can to combat this.

Bland: Often, in winter, canned tomatoes will have more taste than "fresh" tomato-oid objects sold in supermarkets. Cooked tomatoes go nicely with basil, celery seed, ground cloves, oregano, or sage. Of course, if you're making a salad, canned tomatoes are probably not what you want. In that case, add something with zing to your dressing: good mustard, some kind of hot pepper sauce, or grated fresh onion will help.

Difficult to peel: Pour boiling water over the tomatoes and let sit for 3 minutes. Or hold them over an open flame, skewered on a long fork, until the skin breaks. This heat treatment is permanent, so you can boil now and peel later if it suits your purpose.

If you don't want to heat the tomatoes at all, try stroking the skin with the dull edge of a kitchen knife until the skin is all wrinkled. It should come off easily at this juncture. (If it doesn't, perhaps you are at the wrong juncture.)

Green: Green tomatoes will ripen off the vine when wrapped in newspaper and stored in a cool place. They will ripen fairly slowly, however—at least 4 or 5 days from green to red. Wouldn't you rather make tomato pickles (see your cookbook) or perhaps:

GAIL'S SOUTHERN FRIED TOMATOES

Green tomatoes, in thick slices
Salt and pepper
1/2 cup cornmeal
1/2 teaspoon thyme
1 tablespoon brown sugar
Butter

Sprinkle the slices with salt and pepper. Dip in a mixture of cornmeal, thyme, and brown sugar. Fry in butter until brown. Especially good with lamb.

Have one kind, need another: In cooking, 1 cup of canned tomatoes is equivalent to 1½ cups of fresh tomatoes, chopped, then simmered for 10 minutes.

Old: When your fresh tomatoes are getting on in days, try turning them over. Tomatoes will keep longer when stored stem-side down.

Seedy: You may wish to remove the seeds before cooking, since they can make sauces and soups bitter. Cut the tomato in half, and flick the seeds out with the point of a small knife, or use a food mill. For plum tomatoes, cut off the stem end and squeeze the tomato; the seeds should come shooting out.

Too many: You can use tomatoes in dozens of ways at every meal, from tomato omelettes for breakfast to homemade Bloody Marys for a nightcap (put 1 tomato, 1 shot of vodka, and 1 dash of Worcestershire sauce in a blender; blend at high speed for 1 minute). The only important watchword is that tomatoes should never be frozen, as they become hopelessly mushy (at which point they're OK for cooking only).

Unripe: They will ripen faster in a closed brown bag in indirect sunlight.

TOMATO SOUP: *see* SOUPS

TONGUE

Bland: There's not a whole lot you can do with a bland tongue. But you might add four or five whole allspice berries and/or some celery to the cooking water.

Difficult to peel: Add 1 tablespoon of vinegar to the cooking water and cook an additional 10 minutes. Peel while the tongue is hot.

TUNA FISH: *see* FISH AND SEAFOOD

TURKEY: *see* POULTRY

TURNIPS

Bland: So who ever heard of a lively turnip? You can try to liven yours up with either dill seed, dill weed, or poppy seed in the cooking water, and good luck to you.

Old: Old turnips will taste younger and better if you blanch them 5 minutes before cooking. To blanch a turnip, plunge it into a large-enough quantity of boiling water so that the boiling doesn't stop. Leave it in 5 minutes, then proceed as you will. You can blanch your turnips in advance, dipping them in cold water after the 5 minutes to stop the cooking, and use them much later if you wish.

Smelly: Turnips will smell a lot less if you add 1 teaspoon of sugar to the cooking water.

TURNIP GREENS: *see* GREENS

There are very few foods that begin with *U*. In fact, only two come to mind with problems.

UGLI: *see* GRAPEFRUIT *(for peeling or taste concerns with this truly ugly cross between a grapefruit and a tangerine.)*

UPSIDE-DOWN CAKE

Stuck to pan: If the cake has cooled, heat it in the oven and it should flop out on your waiting plate. If it's hopelessly stuck, it will make a wonderful base for a dessert. Spoon the cake into stemmed glasses, or into bowls. Sprinkle it with dessert wine (if you wish) and cover the untidy cake piles with warm pudding of your choice (butterscotch or vanilla work well here) and a dollop of whipped cream. You may never flip an upside-down cake rightside up again.

VEAL

Bland: Consider the addition of these seasonings, all of which do something for veal: allspice, celery seed (sprinkle it on a roast), chervil, cloves (five or six in the gravy), marjoram, oregano, paprika, rosemary, saffron, sage (rub the roast with it), or tarragon.

Not white (tender, succulent) enough: If you have the time, soak the veal in milk overnight in the refrigerator. If you don't have time, blanch the veal briefly.

VEGETABLES: *see specific vegetable*

VEGETABLE SOUP: *see* SOUPS

WAFFLES: *see also* PANCAKES

Stuck to waffle iron: The waffle iron has lost its conditioning, if it ever had it. Now, if the waffles separate, you'll need to pry them out of the top and bottom. Sandwich the two halves together with whipped cream and

jam and call them Belgian Eclair Waffles. They taste great. When the waffle iron is cool, if you no longer want stuck waffles, you'll have to scrub all the stuck-on bits of waffles from the crevices of the waffle iron and brush on cooking oil (corn oil works best). Heat the waffle iron for 10 minutes, turn it off, and let it cool. Then wipe out excess oil with paper towels and vow never to wash your waffle iron—just brush any crumbs out at the end of your waffle session.

WALNUTS: *see* NUTS

WATERMELON

Too much: Mexican cooks know about one of the best things to drink on a hot day. Called *agua fresca* (cold water), it's basically puréed fruit with water and sweetening added. Start with any fruit, but watermelon (or other melon, or berries, or peaches in season—maybe *any* fruit) is particularly good. Remove the rind. Remove seeds by chopping melon into smallish pieces and pressing the fruit through a large-gauge sieve or colander. Purée fruit in a blender or food processor. Thin it out with water if necessary and sweeten. Use some of the Simple Syrup suggested under **PIES, Drying out while cooking**. (This is clearly versatile stuff to keep on hand.) Serve really cold.

WELSH RAREBIT (RABBIT): *see* CHEESE, Cooked cheese that is rubbery, tough, stringy

WHIPPED CREAM: *see also* CREAM

Difficult to whip, won't whip: Chill the cream and the bowl and the beaters. If that doesn't work, add any of the following thickeners: 1 unbeaten egg white, 3 or 4 drops of lemon juice, a pinch of gelatin powder, or a bit of salt sprinkled in, and keep whipping.

Have none, need some: For most uses, you can substitute one mashed banana beaten up with one egg white (beat the egg white stiff first) and sugar to taste. Or use the emergency whipped cream topping, as described in Appendix F.

Old: If you suspect your cream may be getting old and therefore more likely to turn to butter when whipped, add ⅛ teaspoon baking soda per cup of cream before whipping it.

Overwhipped, separated: You'll never have whipped cream, but if you keep on going a bit longer, you'll have delicious homemade butter. Keep beating until it turns solid. Drain off the liquid. Refrigerate until it is hard. Knead it by hand to press out the liquid (which is whey, so now you know what L. M. Muffet was eating with her curds). Now you have sweet butter. If you want salt butter, add ¼ teaspoon salt per pint of cream that you started with, and knead some more.

Won't stay whipped: If you want whipped cream to look right for a long time, as on a dessert or cake that must sit a while, dissolve 1 teaspoon of gelatin in hot milk and beat it into a cup of already-whipped cream.

WIENERS: see SAUSAGES

WINE

Cold: If the wine gets too cold, you'd better use it for cooking; there is no way to warm wine without the flavor being lost.

Sour: You can't de-sour wine, so let it keep on souring, and eventually you'll have some lovely wine vinegar.

YEAST: see also BREAD AND ROLLS, Dough doesn't rise

Expired: Old yeast won't rise. If in doubt, check the expiration date on the package, and, if still unsure, "proof" it by adding a little to warm water with ½ teaspoon of sugar. If it bubbles, it's still good.

Have one kind, need another: 2 tablespoons of dry yeast are equal to a ⅔-ounce cake of compressed yeast.

ZUCCHINI

Overcooked and soggy: There's no going back. You can only go further. Cook it until it's really soft. You're going to make zucchini cream soup. Make a cup of well-seasoned medium white sauce with a good glug of sherry in it. Purée the zucchini (in a blender or a food processor, or even use an electric mixer if it's *really* soggy) and combine with the white sauce. Loosen it to soup consistency with whatever zucchini-cooking fluid there was—cream, milk, or even water. Serve with a little freshly grated nutmeg and a puddle of crème fraîche in the middle of each serving.

Too little: Zucchini combines best with stewed tomatoes, but why not just slice your limited number into thin rounds and use it as a salad ingredient? The next problem is actually more common.

Too much: Home gardeners are wary of the generosity of these plants. If you find yourself ankle-deep in an abundant zucchini harvest, make zucchini bread. It freezes perfectly, keeps for a year in your freezer, and is a splendid accompaniment for hot winter beverages.

FAREWELL ZUCCHINI BREAD

1 cup shredded zucchini
1½ cups flour
1 cup brown sugar
2 teaspoons cinnamon
1 teaspoon baking soda
½ teaspoon baking powder
½ teaspoon salt
2 eggs, slightly beaten
½ cup vegetable oil
1 teaspoon vanilla

Optional:
1 cup chopped nuts
or
½ cup raisins

or
Bits of other dried fruit and
    ½ cup nuts

Preheat oven to 350°. Grease a 5 x 9-inch loaf pan.

Combine dry ingredients. Add the zucchini (and nuts and/or dried fruit if you're using them) and fold and stir until well distributed. Combine the eggs, oil, and vanilla in a small bowl and add all at once to the other ingredients. Combine with a few light folding motions. Put in loaf pan and bake in the middle of the oven. Test for doneness at 1 hour. A toothpick or broomstraw should come out clean when it's done.

This recipe can be made very quickly in a food processor. Dump everything into the bowl and process 5 to 10 seconds with the steel blade. It'll look lumpy, but that's just fine. Bake as above. Be sure the loaves are cool before you wrap them for freezing.

Appendices

Appendix A

Burned Foods

When food burns during cooking, do three things:

1. Stop the food from cooking.

2. Separate the unburned parts from the burned.

3. Treat the unburned parts, if necessary, to prevent a burned taste.

Here is how to do each most effectively:

1. Remove the pot or pan from the heat at once. Fill a container bigger than the pot (use the sink if necessary) with cold water, and put the burned container in the cold water. Speed is of the essence. Just removing a pot from the flame doesn't stop the cooking; the cold-water plunge does.

2. Using a wooden spoon, preferably, remove all ingredients that don't cling, and transfer to another similar container. Be sure you don't scrape or forcibly remove anything—take only what comes easily. (If you now don't have enough of whatever-it-is, see the appropriate alphabetical listing of this book under subheading **Not Enough**.)

3. Taste the food. It is unlikely that it will have a burned taste, but if it does, cover the pot with a damp cloth and let it stand for about ½ hour. Taste it again. If the taste is still unpleasantly burned or smoky, your food is probably beyond repair—unless you can take advantage of the smoky taste by adding barbecue sauce and renaming it "country style" whatever-it-was.

Appendix B

Thawed Frozen Foods

When you defrost frozen foods, either intentionally or accidentally, and you have no need for them right away, most authorities recommend that you do not refreeze; either store them in the refrigerator briefly and use as soon as possible, or throw them out.

The basic question you must now ask yourself is this: How many authorities telling you otherwise would it take to get you to change your mind? One? Ten? A hundred?

We leave this up to you. We do, however, offer the opinion of one reputable authority who says that it is all right to refreeze thawed food. He is Dr. Walter A. Maclinn, a research specialist in food technology at Rutgers University.

Dr. Maclinn says you can expect foods to be somewhat softer than normal when they are thawed the second time, but otherwise everything is all right. This assumes, of course, that the food did not thaw *and* begin to go bad before you refroze it. The package of green beans that mostly defrosted can go back in the freezer. The leftover clam chowder that warmed to room temperature and smells a little bit suspicious should be thrown out.

Appendix C

Too Much Food; How to Store It

This chart gives you an idea of how long leftover foods can survive in the refrigerator or freezer. The times are only approximate, and we make no guarantees, because we don't know how old the food was when you bought it or how close to ideal temperatures your refrigerator performs. (Optimum temperatures are 0° in the freezer and 34° to 38° in the refrigerator.) We tend to be conservative; in most cases, a little bit longer shouldn't hurt. In the Special Notes column, (F) refers to freezer only and (R) to refrigerator only.

KIND OF FOOD	REFRIGERATOR	FREEZER	SPECIAL NOTES
BREAD, CAKES, ROLLS	1–2 days	2 mos.	
DAIRY PRODUCTS			
Butter, margarine	1–2 wks.	3 mos.	(F) Wrap tightly
Cheese:			
Cottage, ricotta	3–5 days	2–3 mos.	Do not freeze creamed cottage cheese or cream cheese. (F) Wrap tightly; cheese may become crumbly.
Other soft cheeses	1–2 wks.	2–3 mos.	
Hard cheeses	3–6 mos.	6 mos.	
Ice cream	2 days	1 mo.	
Milk, cream	3 days	Do not freeze	
EGGS			
Yolks or whites separated, raw	1–2 days	6–8 mos.	(R) Keep yolks covered with water; whites in covered containers.
Whole, raw eggs	7 days	6–8 mos.	(F) Do not freeze in shells. Break into container.
Hard-boiled eggs	8–10 days	Do not freeze	

KIND OF FOOD	REFRIGERATOR	FREEZER	SPECIAL NOTES
FISH			
Cod, flounder, haddock, halibut, shrimp	1 day	4 mos.	(R) Wrap or cover loosely. (F) Wrap tightly in freezer wrap and tape well. Use wax paper to separate individual pieces of fish.
Mullet, ocean perch, sea trout, striped bass, shucked clams	1 day	3 mos.	
Salmon, crab meat	1 day	2 mos.	
Cooked fish, shellfish	1–2 days	3 mos.	
FRUITS			
Citrus fruits, apples	7 days	Do not freeze	(R) Store uncovered or in crisper section
Fruit-juice concentrates	6 days	12 mos.	
All other kinds	3–5 days	10–12 mos.	(F) Fruits other than berries should be packed in sugar or syrup or syrup plus ascorbic acid (vitamin C).
MEATS			
Beef, roasts, steak	3–5 days	12 mos.	(R) Wrap or cover loosely. (F) Wrap tightly in freezer wrap and tape well. Use wax paper to separate individual pieces.
Cooked meat	1–2 days	3 mos.	
Ground meat	1–3 days	1–3 mos.	
Lamb chops	2–3 days	6–7 mos.	
Lamb roasts	5–6 days	6–7 mos.	
Liver, kidneys, tongue	1–2 days	1–3 mos.	

KIND OF FOOD	REFRIGERATOR	FREEZER	SPECIAL NOTES
Pork, cured:			
Bacon	7 days	2–3 mos.	
Frankfurters	7 days	1 mo.	
Ham, sliced	3–5 days	1–2 mos.	
Ham, whole	7 days	1–2 mos.	
Pork, fresh	3–5 days	8 mos.	
Veal, all kinds	3–5 days	6–8 mos.	
POULTRY			
Chicken, cooked	1–2 days	6 mos.	(R) Wrap or cover loosely. (F) Wrap solid pieces tightly in freezer wrap and tape well.
Chicken, pieces	1–2 days	6 mos.	
Chicken, whole	1–2 days	12 mos.	Put cooked juicy dishes in tightly closed, rigid containers.
All other poultry (goose, turkey, duck, etc.)	1–2 days	6 mos.	
SOUPS, STEWS, CASSEROLES	1–2 days	2 mos.	(R) See special hint under **SOUPS, Too much.**
VEGETABLES			
Canned (open); cooked	1–3 days	8–10 mos.	(R) Store canned (open) or cooked vegetables in covered container.
Fresh, aboveground	3–5 days	8–10 mos.	Store fresh vegetables uncovered in crisper section. (F) Boil or blanch before freezing. Do not freeze tomatoes, radishes, or any very crisp vegetables.
Fresh, root	1–2 weeks	8–10 mos.	

Appendix D

Seasonability of Fruits and Vegetables

The simple fact is that fresh fruits and vegetables bought at the peak of their seasons taste a lot better than at other times. With modern hothouse and storage techniques (not to mention air shipment of produce from other parts of the world where the seasons are reversed), many items are available at the market for much longer periods than they used to be, but they are still best in peak season. The following chart shows you when those peak seasons are.

○ = not available　　● = Available　　★ = Peak season

Fruits

	Jan	Feb	Mar	Apr	May	Jun	Jul	Aug	Sep	Oct	Nov	Dec
Apples	●	●	●	●	●	●	●	●	●	★	★	★
Apricots	○	○	○	○	●	★	★	●	○	○	○	○
Avocados	●	●	★	★	●	●	●	●	●	●	●	●
Bananas	●	●	★	★	★	●	●	●	●	●	●	●
Blackberries	○	○	○	○	●	★	★	★	○	○	○	○
Blueberries	○	○	○	○	●	●	★	★	●	○	○	○
Cherries	○	○	○	○	●	★	★	●	○	○	○	○
Cranberries	●	○	○	○	○	○	○	○	●	★	★	●
Grapefruit	★	★	★	★	●	●	●	●	●	●	★	★
Grapes	●	●	●	●	●	●	●	●	★	★	★	●
Lemons	●	●	●	●	●	★	★	●	●	●	●	●
Limes	●	●	●	●	●	★	★	●	●	●	●	●
Melons	○	●	●	●	●	●	★	★	★	★	●	●
Oranges	★	★	★	●	●	●	●	●	●	●	●	★
Peaches	○	○	○	○	○	●	★	★	●	○	○	○
Pears	●	●	●	●	●	●	●	★	★	★	●	●
Persimmons	○	○	○	○	○	○	○	●	★	★	●	●
Pineapples	●	●	★	★	★	★	●	●	●	●	●	●
Quinces	★	●	○	○	○	○	○	○	●	★	★	★
Raspberries	○	○	○	○	●	★	●	●	●	●	○	○
Rhubarb	●	●	●	★	★	★	●	●	●	●	●	●
Strawberries	●	●	●	●	★	★	●	●	●	●	●	●
Tangerines	★	●	●	●	○	○	○	○	○	○	●	★
Watermelons	○	○	○	●	●	★	★	●	●	○	○	○

	Jan	Feb	Mar	Apr	May	Jun	Jul	Aug	Sep	Oct	Nov	Dec

Vegetables

	Jan	Feb	Mar	Apr	May	Jun	Jul	Aug	Sep	Oct	Nov	Dec
Artichokes	●	●	☆	☆	●	○	○	○	○	●	●	●
Asparagus	○	○	●	☆	☆	☆	○	○	○	○	○	○
Beets, greens	●	●	☆	☆	●	●	●	●	○	○	●	●
Broccoli	☆	☆	☆	●	●	●	●	●	●	☆	☆	☆
Brussels sprouts	●	●	●	○	○	○	○	●	●	☆	☆	☆
Cabbage	●	●	●	●	☆	●	●	●	●	●	●	●
Carrots	☆	☆	☆	☆	☆	☆	☆	☆	☆	☆	☆	☆
Cauliflower	●	●	●	●	●	●	●	●	●	☆	☆	●
Celery	☆	☆	☆	☆	☆	☆	☆	☆	☆	☆	☆	☆
Chard	●	●	●	●	●	●	☆	☆	☆	☆	●	●
Chicory	●	●	●	●	●	☆	●	●	●	●	●	●
Collards	☆	●	●	●	●	●	●	●	●	●	●	☆
Corn	●	●	●	●	●	☆	☆	☆	☆	●	●	●
Cucumbers	●	●	●	●	☆	☆	☆	☆	●	●	●	●
Dandelion greens	●	●	☆	☆	☆	☆	●	●	●	●	●	●
Eggplant	●	●	●	●	●	●	●	☆	☆	●	●	●
Endive	☆	☆	☆	●	●	●	●	●	●	●	☆	☆
Escarole	●	●	●	●	●	●	●	●	●	☆	●	●
Green beans	●	●	●	●	☆	☆	☆	☆	●	●	●	●
Green peppers	●	●	●	●	●	●	☆	☆	☆	☆	●	●
Kale	☆	☆	●	●	●	●	●	●	●	●	●	☆
Lettuce	●	●	●	●	●	☆	●	●	●	●	●	●
Lima beans	●	○	●	●	●	●	☆	☆	☆	☆	●	●
Mushrooms	●	●	●	●	●	●	●	●	●	●	☆	☆
Mustard greens	●	●	●	●	●	☆	☆	●	●	●	●	●
Okra	●	●	●	●	●	☆	☆	●	●	●	●	●
Onions, Bermuda	●	●	☆	☆	☆	☆	●	●	●	●	●	●
Onions, green	●	●	●	●	☆	☆	☆	☆	●	●	●	●
Parsnips	☆	☆	☆	☆	☆	☆	☆	☆	☆	☆	☆	☆
Potatoes	☆	☆	☆	☆	☆	☆	☆	☆	☆	☆	☆	☆
Pumpkins	○	○	○	○	○	○	○	○	●	☆	●	○
Radishes	●	●	●	☆	☆	☆	☆	●	●	●	●	●
Rutabagas	☆	☆	☆	●	●	●	●	●	●	☆	☆	☆
Spinach	●	●	☆	☆	☆	☆	●	●	●	●	●	●
Squash, summer	●	●	●	●	☆	☆	☆	●	●	●	●	●
Squash, winter	○	○	○	○	○	○	○	○	●	☆	●	○
Tomatoes	●	●	●	●	●	☆	☆	☆	☆	☆	●	●
Turnips	☆	☆	☆	●	●	●	●	●	●	☆	☆	☆
Watercress	●	●	●	☆	☆	●	●	●	●	●	●	●
Wax beans	●	●	●	●	☆	☆	☆	☆	●	●	●	●

Appendix E

The Art of Measuring:
How to Measure and Pour Foods

When you are following other people's recipes, it is usually wise to use standard measuring spoons and cups, since that is what the recipe maker probably used. (There are exceptions: The story is told of the haughty couple who, having dined out, asked that the chef be presented to them. When he appeared, they asked him, cajoled him, finally even bribed him for the secret of his specialty dish. Finally he gave in. A pinch of this, a handful of that, and so on, he related, and finally, "Just before serving, add one mouthful of wine.")

When you measure dry ingredients (flour, sugar, etc.), heap the cup or spoon to overflowing and then level it off with something flat, like a knife blade or spatula. When measuring sifted flour, always sift before measuring, and never pack the flour into the measuring cup or spoon; that will unsift it.

On the other hand, moist or dense ingredients, like butter and brown sugar, should be packed firmly into the measuring container.

Sticky ingredients, like honey and molasses, should be poured directly into the utensil; never try to dip the utensil into the container. If you grease the cup or spoon lightly, the sticky stuff won't stick.

Weights and Measures You May Need to Know

A. Equivalent Weights and Measures

1 dash = about ⅛ teaspoon

1 teaspoon = ⅓ tablespoon

1 tablespoon = 3 teaspoons

2 tablespoons = ⅛ cup or 1 ounce of liquid

4 tablespoons = ¼ cup

5⅓ tablespoons = ⅓ cup

8 tablespoons = ½ cup

16 tablespoons = 1 cup

1 cup = ½ pint of liquid

1 pint = 2 cups or 16 ounces of liquid

2 pints = 1 quart

4 quarts = 1 gallon

1 pound = 16 ounces

1 jigger of liquid = 1½ ounces = 3 tablespoons of liquid

B. How Much of What Weighs How Much

Bread crumbs: 1 cup = 4 ounces

Butter: 1 stick = 4 ounces = ½ cup

Butter: 2 cups = 1 pound = 4 sticks

Butter: 1 level tablespoon = ½ ounce

Rice: 1 cup = 8 ounces

Sugar: 1 cup granulated = 8 ounces

Sugar: 1 cup brown = 6⅓ ounces

Sugar: 1 cup confectioners' = 5⅓ ounces

C. Can Sizes

6-ounce can = ¾ cup

8-ounce can = 1 cup

No. 1 can = 11 ounces = 1⅓ cups

12-ounce can = 1½ cups

No. 303 can = 16 ounces = 2 cups

No. 2 can = 20 ounces = 2½ cups

No. 2½ can = 28 ounces = 3½ cups

How to Pour

Pouring ingredients from one utensil to another is such a simple thing, and yet it so often results in sugar or oil or milk or whatever all over the counter or the floor.

The main thing you need to know about pouring is funnels. Not necessarily store-bought, fancy plastic or metal funnels, although those are all right, too, but homemade spur-of-the-moment funnels. For example, you carry one around with you all the time: your hand. It takes only a minute of practice to shape your hand into a funnel-like shape, through which you can pour liquids or powders.

Or use paper. Almost any kind of paper, except paper towels, can be rolled up into a temporary funnel—even for liquids. You can pour a whole gallon of liquid through a funnel made from a piece of ordinary writing paper before it starts to get soggy. (Use unprinted paper, if at all possible. Ink is not in any of the basic food groups.) Consider, too, wax paper and aluminum foil.

Here are two laboratory tricks known to all chemists: To pour powders very accurately from a jar, use a rotating, instead of a pouring, motion. Slant the jar or box slightly downward so the contents just fail to come out. Now rotate the jar or box back and forth, from left to right, and you will find you have amazingly accurate control over how much comes out.

To pour liquids from a large unwieldy can, where the hole or spout is not centered (as with big cans of oil, for example), pour with the spout at the top—that is, as far as possible from the container you are pouring into. This results in a steadier flow, less dripping, and a neater "cutoff" when you stop pouring.

Appendix F

A Last Resort Dinner

Here is a quite satisfactory meal for four persons, made up entirely of items of the "first-aid" list given on page xv. It should take about 20 to 25 minutes from the time you discover your regular dinner is ruined until you sit down at the table.

Menu

Sherried Seafood on Biscuits
Artichoke Heart Salad
Poached Fruit in Vanilla Sauce with Whipped Topping

INGREDIENTS

Biscuit mix
1 12-oz. can evaporated milk
2 cans shrimp
1 can clam chowder
3 tablespoons sherry
$\frac{1}{2}$ teaspoon pepper
1 can quartered artichoke hearts
3 tablespoon strips of sun-dried tomatoes
1 large can pears or peaches
Paprika

OPTIONAL:

Whole milk
Flour
Canned hollandaise sauce
Butter
Sugar
Fresh vegetables for garnish

First, heat the oven to the temperature given on the biscuit-mix box. While the oven is heating, open your can of evaporated milk and put $\frac{1}{2}$ cup of it into a bowl you can whip it up in. Put the bowl and your beaters (whether electric or hand) into the freezer for later.

Now make the biscuit dough following the recipe on the box. If your emergency evaporated milk is the only milk you have, make the biscuits using water. The topping is rich enough that it won't matter all that much. Don't bother to roll out perfect rounds, however; they'll be buried under shrimp. Instead, divide the dough into heaps (two per person) on a floured board. You can use biscuit mix if you're out of flour. Roll each heap into a rough ball and flatten it gently until ½ inch thick. Put them on a greased cookie sheet and into the oven.

While the biscuits are baking, open the 2 cans of shrimp, dump them into a strainer or colander and rinse them under cold running water. Set them to drain. Put the clam chowder in a saucepan over low heat. Mix the remaining evaporated milk with an equal amount of water (no need to be exact about this) and measure out the amount you'll need for the vanilla pudding sauce—½ cup less than the pudding directions call for. Dump the rest of the milk into the chowder and stir it in. Stir in the shrimp, 1 tablespoon of sherry, and ½ teaspoon of pepper. Now you have to use your judgment. If the creamed shrimp is too thick, thin it out with a little water (or milk, or cream, if you have it; even sour cream will work just fine). Keep warm over low heat.

Now make the vegetable. Drain the artichoke hearts, slice them into eighths, and put the slices in a bowl. Cut the sun-dried tomatoes into thin strips. Toss the tomato strips and artichoke hearts with a sharp vinaigrette dressing. Put in the fridge to chill.

Now start making the dessert. Drain the fruit and put it in a saucepan. Mix up the instant vanilla pudding using ½ cup less milk than the instructions on the box call for. Add 2 tablespoons of sherry, pour it over the fruit and set it over very low heat to warm.

By now the biscuits are ready. Split them. Butter them, if you wish, but it's not necessary. Top them with the creamed shrimp. Do you have anything fresh you can garnish this with? Parsley? A wedge of tomato? A few snippets of green onion? No? How about a shake of paprika, then?

Serve with the artichoke heart salad.

You'll have to get up in 10 minutes and turn off the fruit. Cover it and let it just sit there until you're ready for it. When you are, make the topping by whipping the well-chilled evaporated milk. When it's at the soft peak stage, beat in 3 rounded tablespoons of sugar, if you have it. Divide the fruit into serving dishes, spoon on the topping, and serve at once.

Congratulations. You have just survived a total disaster.

Appendix G

Stains

Here are suggestions on how to remove the most common food and food-related stains. On colored fabrics, it is always safest to treat an inconspicuous area with the cleaning solution before removing the entire stain.

Alcoholic beverages: Sponge with amyl acetate (banana oil) or cleaning fluid. Launder in hot water, and rinse in warm water.

Blood: Soak in cold water. Wash in warm water. If stain remains, soak in ammonia water (2 tablespoons per gallon).

Chocolate, cocoa: Soak in cold water; sponge in hot sudsy water. Bleach with hydrogen peroxide if necessary. Wash in hot water (warm for colored fabrics).

Coffee, tea: Pour boiling water through stain. Launder normally. If stain remains, bleach with hydrogen peroxide.

Egg: Soak in cold water; never hot. Launder normally with hot water. For colored fabrics, if colorfast, soak in solution of 2 tablespoons detergent and 1 tablespoon hydrogen peroxide per gallon of water. Launder normally with warm water.

Fruits: Rinse in cold running water; wash in hot water with detergent. If stain remains, bleach with hydrogen peroxide.

Grease on carpet: Pour on club soda. Rub with a clean cloth or damp sponge.

Lipstick: Rub with lard, and blot until stain is transferred to blotter. Wash in hot water (warm for colored fabrics) with detergent. Bleach with hydrogen peroxide if necessary.

Meat, gravy: Soak in cold water, never hot. Wash with hot water (warm for colored fabrics) and detergent. Bleach with hydrogen peroxide if necessary.

Milk, cream, ice cream: Rinse under cold running water. Wash in hot water (warm for colored fabrics) with detergent.

Mustard: Work glycerin in; rub spot; then wash in hot water (warm for colored fabrics) with detergent. If stain remains, bleach with hydrogen peroxide.

Soft drinks: Sponge with equal parts of alcohol and glycerin, or with lukewarm water and alcohol. Launder in hot water (warm for colored fabrics) and detergent.

Vegetables: Rinse in cold running water. Wash in hot water with detergent (warm for colored fabrics). If stain remains, bleach with hydrogen peroxide.

Appendix H

Problems with Utensils and Appliances

Look first for the kind of utensil or appliance, like *Pot* or *Grinder,* and then for the kind of problem, like **Burned** or **Clogged**.

Aluminumware

Dirty: Boil apple peels in aluminum pots; it will make cleaning them (the pots) ever so much easier. It's some chemical miracle at work.

Stained or darkened: Boil 2 teaspoons of cream of tartar in 1 quart of water for 10 minutes to lighten darkened aluminum.

Bottles

Dirty: If the bottle brush won't reach or isn't strong enough, fill the bottle halfway with soapy water and add a handful of pea-sized pebbles. Shake vigorously. Save the pebbles for another time. If you're afraid of breaking the bottle, you might try using split peas or other dried beans instead of pebbles. If you have a sack of those ceramic pie weights, the ones that look like tiny smooth chickpeas, you can use them.

Smelly: Fill bottle half full of water. Add 1 tablespoon of mustard or baking soda. Shake well, and let stand for 1 hour; then rinse.

Coffee or Tea Strainer

Clogged: Sprinkle coarse salt in the basket and run under hot water.

Cutting Board

Smelly: Rub it with a sliced lemon or lime.

Dishes or Plates

Cracked: For hairline cracks, put the plate in a pan of milk and boil for 45 minutes. The crack will usually disappear; if not, it was probably bigger than you thought.

Greasy: Hot soak them with baking soda in water. Chemically, baking soda plus grease equals soap. Not soap you'd use on the baby, but nevertheless soap that will clean your dishes.

Smelly: Wash them in salty water. Or use a little ammonia in hot soapy water. Or add a bit of ground mustard to the wash water.

Stained: Soak them overnight in hot soda water. (That's hot water plus baking soda.) Then rub with a vinegar-moistened cloth dipped in salt. This is especially effective on tea stains.

Enamelware

Dirty: Fill with cold water plus 3 tablespoons of salt. Let sit overnight. Then boil. Then clean (easily).

Forks

Dirty: Try cleaning them with an old toothbrush. (Dirty toothbrush? Try cleaning it with an old fork.)

Freezer or Fridge

Not working: You've probably heard that you lose half an hour of safe cool temperature every time you open the door. Consider putting really perishable things (like cream, which you're likely to use more often) into an ice chest, if you have one.

Garbage Disposal

Smelly: Grind up half a lemon, orange, or grapefruit in it. In fact, never throw a lemon rind out—keep them in quarters in a plastic bag in your freezer and throw one down the disposal whenever it begins to smell funny.

Glass Bakeware

Things stick to it: Lower the heat you use when you cook in glass by 25° and increase the cooking time slightly.

Glassware

Stained: If the stains are coffee stains, make tea in the utensil; the tannic acid of the tea should remove the coffee stains.

Stuck together (glasses): Put cold water in the top one and sink the bottom one in hot water. They will come apart.

Grater

Smelly: Rub a hard crust of bread over it.

Griddle

Smoking: This hint alone is worth the price of the book. This may be the most useful hint ever devised. This is the kind of hint that will make you want to drop everything and call up all your friends and relations and share it with them before another minute goes by. Are you ready? All right, here it is: To keep your griddle from smoking, rub it regularly with half a rutabaga. (Applause?)

Grinder

Clogged: Rub it with half a rutabaga. No. Wait. Ignore that; we were just overcome with emotion from the last hint. What you really do is insert crumpled wax paper and keep grinding away. The paper will force every last bit of food through but won't go through itself or jam up the works.

Dirty: Run a piece of bread through it before you wash it.

Hands (your very own)

Burned: Vanilla extract will help take away the initial pain; so will a paste of baking soda and water. So will a good stiff shot of bourbon.

Greasy: Very hot water will generally dissolve and remove most food-type grease. Next time, for greasing baking pans and the like, wear a wax-paper or plastic-wrap bag as a glove to smear the butter around with.

Smelly: One of the finest household hints devised by man (are you listening, Heloise?) was announced by Hank Weaver on his commentary program of radio station KABC in Los Angeles in 1956. It went as follows: "Ladies, to get that ugly onion smell off your hands once and for all, simply rub them with garlic."

Slightly more reputable methods of de-onionizing your hands are the following: (1) wash with cold water, rub hands with salt and rinse; (2) rub hands with celery salt and wash normally; (3) rub with a raw, unpeeled potato; (4) wash with milk, then with cold water.

For fishy-odored hands, dampen them, rub with salt, wash normally, and then rub with a lemon rind. (If this doesn't work, have you considered the possibility that your hands just naturally smell like fish?)

Stained: There are two ways to get off most fruit and some vegetable stains. One is to rub the stain with a raw potato, unpeeled, and then wash normally. The other, best with acid fruit stains but good for many others as well, is to wash the hands, wipe lightly, strike a match, and cup your hands around the match to catch the smoke. Stains vanish as if by magic, leaving only clean, blistered (if you keep them there too long) hands.

Ironware

Greasy: Pour in lots of salt, and you can easily wipe up grease plus salt with paper towels.

Rusting: Immerse in turpentine for anywhere from 1 hour to 3 days, depending on how much rust. Then scour with steel wool. You'll have to break the ironware in all over again.

Jars: see Screw-Top Containers

Kitchen

Smelly: For an inexpensive and delightful kitchen deodorizer, put some orange peel in the oven at 350°, with the door ajar. If you've got a really powerful odor you need to deal with fast, boil a teaspoonful of cloves in a mixture of 1 cup water with ¼ cup of vinegar—but be careful not to let the liquid boil away, or you'll be dealing with the smell of burned cloves.

Knives

Rusting: Stick them through an onion and leave them there for ½ hour, then wash and polish them. Wipe them with a very light coating of vegetable oil to keep the rust from returning.

Meat Grinder: see Grinder

Microware Oven

Smelly: Chop half a lemon into four pieces. Put them in a small bowl with 1 cup of water and a few whole cloves. Boil for 5 minutes.

Omelette Pan

Sticky: Presumably you have seasoned your omelette pan following the manufacturer's instructions. Don't use soap and water on it now. Pour a small mound of salt in it and scrub it with a paper towel moistened in cooking oil. Wipe it out with another paper towel. This is actually the best way to clean a wok, too.

Oven

Dirty: Sprinkle a combination of salt and cinnamon on any spillovers that occur while baking. Not only does it prevent a burned, smoky smell from filling the house, but you should be able to use a spatula to lift the boil-over in one big ugly piece after the oven cools.

Does not heat: Many things that are made in the oven can be adapted to stove-top cooking (assuming the stove top works. If it doesn't, *see* **STOVE TOP, Does not heat** for further suggestions). Anything you were planning to roast can be cut up and braised over low heat or sliced thin and sautéed. If you have more things that need cooking or heating than you have burners for, cook things in layers: Put a bowl with cooked food (or something that just needs heating) over a pot boiling something else. Steam vegetables in a colander suspended over a pot with boiling potatoes in it. If you were planning a cake for dessert, turn it into a steamed pudding—which can be basically a cake steamed in a covered bowl. Consult your big cookbook for exact directions.

Temperature unknown: (And you have no thermometer to check it.) How could this possibly happen? Okay—the knob falls apart. Now what you do is preheat the oven for 15 minutes. Put a sheet of plain white paper on the center rack. Leave it in for 5 minutes. Check the color:

pale biscuit color: 300° or less

light brown: 350 to 400°

golden brown: 400 to 450°

deep brown: 450 to 500°

black: over 500°

ashes: don't even use it for pizza!

Pans: *see Pots and Pans*

Pastry Tips

Clogged: Metal ones can be boiled clean. Plastic ones must be soaked in hot water. Ream them out with a wooden toothpick or a bamboo skewer.

Pitcher

Drippy: If you're sure someone hasn't given you one of those dribble pitchers from the joke shop, you can quell drips by rubbing the top of the lip of the pitcher with a tiny bit of butter. There's a tongue twister in there somewhere, but we can't quite find it.

Plasticware

Stained: Soak for 20 minutes in a gallon of warm water plus 1 cup of bleach. Wipe the plasticware dry and then wash it normally. If this doesn't work, rub the stains with dry baking soda. If that doesn't work, sand the plastic with a very fine grade of silicon carbide paper (the black stuff that feels like sandpaper). Be sure the plastic is wet when you sand it.

Plastic Wrap

Stuck: Some people, discouraged by the failure of the plastic-wrap people to come up with a product where you can always find the end when you want it, have taken to keeping their plastic wrap in the refrigerator. Cold plastic wrap is easier to handle and just as effective.

Plates: *see* Dishes or Plates

Pots and Pans

Burned: For aluminum, iron, ceramic, Pyrex, and stainless pots and pans, first scrape out what you can with a wooden spoon. Then partly fill with water and a strong detergent. Boil for 10 minutes. Let stand as is overnight. Then pour off the water, and the burned part will be cleanable with a scouring pad or steel wool. (Alternate method: Add lots of salt to the contents, and heat on the stove; the food may "flake" out along with the salt.)

For aluminum pans, the following miracle can often be worked: Boil an onion in the pan, and the burned stuff will detach itself and rise to the top.

If a truly beloved utensil is "hopelessly" burned, there are professionals who specialize in restoring such items. They clean them with strong acid and repolish the metal. This will cost more than buying a new one, but if it was the pot you cooked the goulash in that caused your spouse to propose to you, it may be worth it. Check the Yellow Pages under "Metal Finishers." These are the same people who can re-coat the inside of heavy copper pans that have a silvery-colored lining that, over the years, has worn off. Since good quality copper pots are exceedingly expensive, their repair often makes good sense.

Dirty: Some kinds of dirt are best cleaned in cold water, not hot. These include eggs, dough, sauces, and puddings.

Greasy: As you may have read under **Dishes or Plates, Greasy,** hot-soaking them with baking soda in the water works best. Chemically, baking soda plus grease equals soap.

Rusting: This works especially well with cake pans: Scour them with a hunk of raw potato dipped in cleaning powder.

Smelly: Wash them in salt water or in hot soapy water plus a dash of ammonia.

Refrigerator: see Freezer or Fridge

Scissors

Dull: Cut a piece of sandpaper into strips. You'll not only have a lovely collection of narrow strips of sandpaper; you'll have a sharper pair of scissors.

Screw-Top Containers

Stuck: H. Allen Smith revealed to the world the technique for opening all screw-top containers. Now there are untold millions of us who face Mount Kisco or wherever he lived and say "thank you" every time we are faced with an obstinate top. The technique: Bang the top *flatly* on a hard surface, like the floor. Not the edge, but the flat surface of the top. Just once. Hard. That's all. And to think of all those jars we used to hold under hot water.

Stainless Steel

Stained: This is like giving instructions for ironing permanent-press fabrics. Nonetheless, if you have rainbow-like stains on your stainless steel, they are permanent; they will never come out. For brownish stains, soak a dishcloth in full-strength ammonia, cover the stain with it for 30 minutes, and wash normally.

Stove Top

Does not heat: This is often a last-minute discovery that calls for real ingenuity. What else do you have in your household that does heat? Toasters, electric skillets, toaster ovens, slow cookers, and deep-fat fryers (which can be used for soup or stews or boiling water—just make sure you clean it well before you use it). Have you a camp stove? Could you use a barbecue or hibachi? Could your fireplace be used? (This is getting adventurous.) Warm bread or rolls in the drying cycle of a dishwasher—being very careful about the setting when you turn it on. And we have been told that it is possible to strap a foil-wrapped chicken to the exhaust manifold of a car and drive until it's done—but as long as you're out in the car, why not head for a restaurant?

Teflon

Stained: In the utensil, boil a mixture of 1 cup water, ½ cup bleach, and 2 tablespoons baking soda. Then wash in warm suds. Re-coat the Teflon with oil before using it.

Thermos Bottles

Dirty: Fill with warm water plus 1 heaping teaspoon of baking soda. Let sit overnight; then clean.

Woodenware

Worn-out: If it is really worth saving, here's how: Sand thoroughly. Then make a mixture of 1 tablespoon mineral oil and ½ tablespoon of powdered pumice (from the hardware store). Rub on the wood with cheesecloth until it is dry and smooth—perhaps ½ hour. Let dry for 24 hours. Remove the dust. Repeat this operation if necessary. It could take ten or twelve times to restore a really battered wooden item. Never, never wax, shellac, or polish a good wooden bowl.

Your Own Tips Journal

_____
_____
_____
_____
_____
_____
_____
_____
_____
_____
_____
_____
_____
_____
_____
_____
_____
_____
_____
_____
_____
_____